Jews in Blue

Jews in Blue

The Jewish American Experience
in Law Enforcement

Jack Kitaeff

CAMBRIA
PRESS

Youngstown, New York

This book has been registered with the Library of Congress.
Kitaeff, Jack
        Jews in Blue / Jack Kitaeff
        p. cm.

    Includes bibliographical references
     ISBN10: 1-934043-04-4
     ISBN13: 978-1-934043-04-2

For My Father

Table of Contents

Introduction

Contrary to popular belief, it was not Queen Isabella's jewelry, but Spanish Jewry that made Columbus' historical trip to the New World possible. If the Spanish Jew Luis de Santangel had not lent Isabella the money to finance the voyage, there would have been no New Amsterdam a century-and-half later, no Jewish policeman posted as part of the official Night Guard, and no America at all.

Fortunately, Columbus set sail in 1492 bringing with him the first influx of Jewish people to North America. Although by the time Isabella expelled the Jews, things had become intolerable for Spain's Jewry, this was not always the case in earlier years.

The Jews had a long and extensive history in Spain and it is believed that Jews lived there since the era of King Solomon. In 409 CE, the Visigoths (Aryan Christians) conquered Spain and treated the Jews terribly. For example, a canon was passed in 589 prohibiting the marriage of Jews and non-Jews, and in 612, the Council of Toledo ordered the baptism of all Jews.

The situation for Jews improved somewhat in 711 CE when Spain fell under the rule of the Muslim Moors. Both Muslims and Jews built a civilization, based in the city of Cordoba, also known as Al-Andalus, which was more advanced than any civilization in Europe at that time. Jews were able to coexist peacefully with their neighbors, and were allowed to practice their religion, however, they were required to pay a special tax, the "jizha."

This era of Muslim rule in Spain (8th-11th century) was considered the "Golden Age" for Spanish Jewry. Jewish intellectual and spiritual life flourished and many Jews served in Spanish courts. Jewish economic expansion was unparalleled. In Toledo, Jews were involved in translating Arabic texts to the various romance languages, as well as translating Greek and Hebrew texts into Arabic. Jews also contributed to botany, geography, medicine, mathematics, poetry and philosophy.

Jews for the most part were still made to live separately from Christians in aljamas (Jewish quarters). They were given administrative control over their communities and managed their own communal affairs. Jews had their own court system, known as the Bet Din. Rabbis served as judges and rendered both religious and civil legal opinions.

But change was in the wind for Spanish Jews when Christians conquered Toledo in 1098 CE. At first the Jews continued to be involved in the cultural, economic, intellectual, financial and political life of Christian Spain. By the mid-13th century, however, the Christians controlled most of Spain and increasingly forced Jews to convert to Christianity. In 1391, persecution of Jews became violent and intolerably oppressive, thousands of Jews were killed in riots, synagogues were seized and turned into churches and holy books were stolen or censored. They were ready to leave.

The creation of the United States as a democracy 380 years later, was rooted in the Hebrew Bible. Many of the earliest pilgrims who settled the "New England" of America in the early 17th century were Puritan refugees escaping religious persecutions in Europe. These Puritans viewed their emigration from England as a virtual re-enactment of the Jewish exodus from Egypt. To them, England was Egypt, the king was Pharaoh, the Atlantic Ocean was the Red Sea, America was the Land of Israel, and the Indians were the ancient Canaanites. They were the new Israelites, entering into a new covenant with God in a new Promised Land. Indeed, the "American" holiday of Thanksgiving, first celebrated in 1621, a year after the Mayflower landed, was initially conceived of as a day parallel to the Jewish Day of Atonement, Yom Kippur; it was to be a day of fasting, introspection and prayer.

There would have been few Jews in the English Colonies if it had not been for Rabbi Manasseh Ben Israel of Amsterdam, Holland. A four hundred year old law forbade Jews from settling on English land. Rabbi Manasseh addressed Oliver Cromwell, Lord Protector of England, arguing that England must allow Jews to live on its soil or else the Day of Judgment will never come for Christian or Jew. The ban was revoked. The influence of Jews on the development of the United States' government and political system is monumental. President John Adams acknowledged this when he said, "The Jews have done more to civilize men than any other nation. They are the most glorious nation that ever inhabited the earth. The Romans and their Empire were but a bauble in comparison to the Jews. They have given religion to three-quarters of the Globe and have influenced the affairs of Mankind more happily than any other nation, ancient or modern" (American Jewish Archives, 2005).

An early example of the influence of Jewish ideas took place in the Continental Congress when Thomas Jefferson, Benjamin Franklin and John Adams were creating a great seal. Among the suggested logos was one found in Jefferson's papers depicting the Israelites and Moses standing on the shore while Pharaoh and his army drown in the Red Sea. The encircling phrase reads "Rebellion to Tyrants is Obedience to God." This was a powerful metaphor depicting the American patriots as latter day Israelites fighting the tyranny of the contemporary Egyptians, the British.

Despite these facts (and for whatever reasons), many people today do not acknowledge the significant role that Jews have played in the formative years of this country. Perhaps as a response to this historical myopia, there are a good number of books on the market depicting Jewish-American history and the influence that various great Jewish-Americans have had in the last few centuries.

Looking over the books describing Jewish contributions, their themes are many. These include Jews in government, science, medicine, law, business, and even sports. My goal in writing this book is to explore an area which is almost never described as having a Jewish influence – police work and law enforcement.

This first chapter of this book, "Shomrim," begins with Columbus and the Jews aboard his ship as they land in the New World. I will explore the resistance and disdain displayed to Jews by Peter Stuyvesant under Spanish rule, and I will usher in the appearance of The first Jewish policeman, Asser Levy in 1654.

The first society of Jewish policemen called Shomrim ("guardian" or "watcher") will be examined from its development in 1924 by Captain Jacob Kaminsky of the New York City Police Department, when there were only a handful of Jews in the Department, through Shomrim's growth period in the post-depression years when its numbers exploded in the NYPD as civil service jobs became attractive in difficult economic times.

In chapter two, "Should a Jew be a Cop?" I will look at whether police work is a logical career for Jews from a Biblical, moral, and historical perspective.

In chapter three, "Feds," I will present biographical sketches of some of this Country's most prominent Jews in federal law enforcement. These include the first Jewish federal officer, Reuben Etting, who was appointed by Thomas Jefferson; Edward H. Levi, the only Jewish United States Attorney General; Michael Chertoff, head of Homeland Security, and the son of a rabbi; and the first woman (or Jew) to be the head of the United States Drug Enforcement Administration, Karen Tandy.

In the fourth chapter, "New York," notable high-ranking Jewish police officers from New York State will be profiled. These include New York City's first chief of police, Jacob Hays; the NYPD's flamboyant Chief of Detectives from the 1970s, Al Seedman; the NYPD's only Jewish Police Commissioner ever, Howard Safir; and the first women to be promoted to sergeant in the NYPD, Felicia Shpritzer and Gertrude Schimmel.

In chapter five, "California," I concentrate on famous and prominent law enforcement officials from that state. These include the only Jewish chief of police ever of the Los Angeles Police Department, Emil Harris; the Sheriff of San Diego County, Bill Kalender; and the San Diego District Attorney, Bonnie Dumanis.

Chapter six, "Special Cases," will discuss Jewish law enforcement officers who may not fit the "typical" Jews in blue mold. These include Reuben Greenberg, the nation's only Jewish African-American chief of police; a cop turned rabbi, a rabbi turned cop, the first police officer who was simultaneously a psychologist, the nation's only Hassidic police officer, and a famous Jew in blue who was also known as the "King of Rock and Roll."

Sources

Adams, John. 2005. American Jewish Archives. http://american jewisharchives.com (acquired November 27, 2005).

chapter 1
Shomrim: the Jewish Watchmen

"Thou shalt not stand idly by thy neighbor's blood,"
– Leviticus 9:16.

In the summer of 1947, testifying before the UN Commission Regarding the Partition of Palestine, David Ben-Gurion spoke these words:

> About 300 years ago a ship named the Mayflower set sail to the New World. It was an important event in the annals of England and America, yet I wonder if there is even one Englishman who knows exactly when that ship set sail, and how many Americans know how many people were on that ship? And what type of bread did they eat when they left England? Yet more than 3,300 years ago, before the Mayflower, set sail, the Jews left Egypt. And every Jew in the world knows exactly on what day they left: They left on the 15th of Nisan. And everyone knows what kind of bread they ate: They ate matzo. And until today Jews all over the world eat matzo on the 15th of Nisan and recount the Exodus . . . that is the nature of the Jews (American Jewish Archives, 2005).

Ben-Gurion may have been using history to point out the strong commitment and sense of history and tradition of the Jewish people. He may also have been illustrating that for Jews, all the elements of our collective experience have become archetypal and enduring components of Jewish identity to this day. All this makes history very important for Jews, and the history of the first Jews in North America very important for the identity of American Jewry, American Jews in law enforcement, and for America as a whole. It is important, therefore, to be aware of the circumstances which brought Jews to the North American continent in the 15th and 16th century. Many of these circumstances can be traced back to the horrible events of the Inquisition.

By the year 280 CE the Inquisition had become a well-established, brutal, and permanent institution in the Catholic Church. Those who had religious beliefs or engaged in practices which were not in line with Church orthodoxy were openly persecuted. Church Councils required secular rulers to prosecute all heretics, and in 1231, Pope Gregory IX published a decree which called for life imprisonment for anyone who had confessed and repented, and death for those heretics who persisted in their ways.

In as much as the Inquisition was the official law of the Papal empire, each region in the empire had a system established to help it function. There was a judge or inquisitor who could bring suit against anyone. A judge had to be at least forty years old, of unimpeachable reputation, distinguished for virtue and wisdom, a master of canon law, and a follower of all ecclesiastical rules and regulations. An accused person was forced to testify against himself and did not have any right to face or question his accuser. It was acceptable for judges to take testimony from criminals, persons of bad reputation, excommunicated people, and other "heretics." There was no right to counsel and sentences were final and could not be appealed.

Sometimes inquisitors interrogated entire populations in their jurisdiction. An accused was given a summary of the charges and had to take an oath to tell the truth. Judges and inquisitors used any means necessary to obtain confessions including torture. Death sentences were by burning at the stake and it was carried out by the secular authorities. These executions became public spectacles and were known as "auto da fe" where the condemned apostates were burned alive.

It was against this historical backdrop that at midnight on August 2, 1492, it became illegal for Jews to remain on Spanish soil. On August 3, 1492 Columbus set sail on his expedition and it is generally accepted that accompanying Columbus on his voyage were several Jews, including, arguably, Columbus himself. By the time New Amsterdam was founded in 1624, thousands of Jews had settled in the Americas. Most of these early colonists were Sephardic Jews and came from places such as Brazil and Portugal. One of the many Portuguese Jews who had escaped the Inquisition to the North American continent was Asser Levy. In 1657, Levy applied to become one of the first members of the Night Watch established by the Dutch to protect New Amsterdam. The watch consisted of eight paid guards who carried large wooden rattles. These rattles made an extremely loud noise and were used to alert the citizens in the event of danger. These watchmen were, in essence, the first paid police officers in New York City history.

Peter Stuyvesant, as Governor and director of the Burgher Guard (formally known as the Rattle Watch), set forth regulations for all new watchman. These were listed in Augustine Costello's *Our Police Protectors, History of the New York Police*, and include:

1. Watchmen to be on duty before bell-ringing, under penalty of six stivers.
2. Whoever stays away without sending a substitute, to be fined two guilders for benefit of the regular watch.
3. [A Watchman is to be fined] one guilder fine for drunkenness.
4. [A Watchman is to be fined] ten stivers fine for sleeping on post.
5. If any arms are stolen through negligence of the watch, the watchman to pay for the arms and be fined one guilder for the first, two guilders for the second, and the fine for the third offense to be discretionary with the court.
6. [A Watchman will be fined] two guilders for going away from the watch, and one guilder for missing turn.
7. The Watch to call the hour at all corners from 9 A.M. until reveille, for which they received an additional compensation of eighteen guilders per month.

8. If any one, on the Burgher guard, take the name of God in vain, he shall forfeit for the first offense ten stivers; for the second, twenty stivers; and for the third time, twenty stivers.

9. Whosoever on the Burgher guard speaks ill of a comrade shall forfeit thirty stivers.

10. Whosoever comes fuddled or intoxicated on guard, shall, for each offense, pay twenty stivers; whosoever is absent from his watch, without lawful reason, shall forfeit fifty stivers.

11. After the watch is duly performed and daylight is come, and the reveille beaten, whosoever discharges his gun or musket without orders of his Corporal shall pay one guilder (U.S. Geneological Network, 2005).

The *Jewish Encyclopedia* lists the rules of the Burgher Guard under Stuyvesant, which had a clear Christian tone.

Whereas, we have observed and remarked the insolence of some of our inhabitants, who are in the habit of getting drunk, of quarreling, fighting and of smiting each other on the Lord's Day of Rest (of which, on the last Sunday, we ourselves witnessed the painful scenes, and to the knowledge of which we came by report) in defiance of the magistrates, to the contempt and disregard of our person and authority, to the great annoyance of the neighborhood, and finally to the injury and dishonoring of God's holy laws, and commandments, which enjoin upon us to honor and sanctify him on this, His Holy Day of Rest, and which proscribe all personal injury and murder, with the means and temptations that may lead thereunto (Jewish Encyclopedia, 2005).

Therefore, by the advice of His Excellency, the Director-General, and our ordained Council, here present, to the end that we may, so far as it is possible and practicable, take all

due care and prevent the curse of God instead of His bless-
ing from falling upon us and our good inhabitants, do, by these
presents, charge, command, and enjoin upon all tapsters and
innkeepers, that on the Sabbath of the Lord, commonly called
Sunday, before two of the clock in the afternoon, in case
there is no preaching, or otherwise, before four of the clock
(in the afternoon) they shall not be permitted to set, nor draw,
nor bring out for any person or persons, any wines, beers, nor
any strong waters of any kind whatsoever, on whatever pretext,
excepting only persons traveling and the daily boarders that
may from necessity be confined to their places of abode, in
the penalty of being deprived of their occupations, and, over
than, in the penalty of six Carolus guilders for each person
that during said time may or shall have run up a score for
wine or beer in their house (p. 268).

Levy's application was rejected by Peter Stuyvesant. In Stuyvesant's
letter declining Levy's service, he stressed that Levy was part of a
"deceitful race" who are "hateful enemies and blasphemers of the
name of Christ" and should not be allowed to "further infect and
trouble this new colony" (American Jewish Archives, 2005).

Stuyvesant's decision was overruled by the Dutch West India
Company and Levy and the other Jews were allowed to serve on the
Burgher Guard. On April 21, 1657, Levy became one of the first
Jewish police officers in America – and the first Shomer.

Thanks to the efforts of Asser Levy, by the middle of the seven-
teenth century, Jews in New Amsterdam had acquired definite rights,
and the municipal authorities began to treat them more fairly. For
example, on Nov. 15, 1727, an act was passed by the General Assem-
bly of New York providing that when an oath was to be taken by any
one of His Majesty's (i.e., British) subjects who professed the Jewish
religion, the words "upon the true faith of a Christian" could be omitted.

Shomrim in the Hebrew means "guardian," or "watcher." The early
Shomrim societies in the United States were at first organized to be

guardians against discrimination of Jewish police officers. But in Biblical times, "Shomrim" were the sentries that guarded Jewish camps, fortresses, and villages. By choosing to become a Guardian or Shomer, one committed to standing guard for those who might be vulnerable and at risk.

The first Shomrim Society in the United States was established by members of the New York City Police Department in 1924 and Captain Jacob Kaminsky was the Society's first president. Other fraternal and charitable organizations (such as the Emerald Society for Irish officers within the police department) had long since existed.

There was not exactly a pressing need to establish a Shomrim Society in the NYPD in 1924 as only 1% of the New York City Police Department was Jewish. The "spark" which finally motivated the formation of the society may have been an off-color remark made to a young Jewish officer to the effect that "he might feel more at home with a salami than a nightstick."

The ranks of the Shomrim Society swelled in the NYPD during the depression and post-depression eras of the 1930s and 1940s as civil service jobs provided the only secure means of making a living for many men in such troubling economic times. Indeed, the civil service lists of 1935-37 added 400 new Shomrim members. In 1939, 33,000 men took the police test and only 1440 did well enough to pass. About one-third of the men who passed the test were Jews. Most of these men were college graduates, many were laid off teachers, out of work lawyers or accountants, and two were even physicians. This graduating recruit class of 1940 would eventually move on to fill such positions as Chief Inspector, Bureau Chief, and Chief of the Narcotics Division.

One of the prime movers in the NYPD Shromin Society and also a graduate of the famous 1940 police academy class was Lou Weiser who is today affectionately known as "Mr. Shomrim."

For Lou and others in his Brooklyn neighborhood in 1939, the lure of a steady job was the impetus to take the police test. He admits that police work was not something he or anyone else he grew up with had ever even considered. But even the low pay and long hours of being a patrolman was better than the prospect of no work at all.

Weiser started his career at the 72 Precinct in Brooklyn, South and soon was assigned to the Detective Bureau's Brooklyn West Youth Squad due to his command of "Yiddish." After being promoted to detective he was transferred to the 61 Precinct Detective Squad and remained there after being promoted to sergeant. After becoming a lieutenant, Weiser was assigned to the 112 Precinct and later to the Department of Investigation (DOI) where he eventually served as Assistant Commissioner until his retirement in 1965.

Although he had numerous accomplishments on the police department, Weiser is particularly known for having been involved in the investigation and arrest of Willie Sutton.

Willie Sutton was born on June 30, 1901, in Brooklyn, New York. He attended school through eighth grade and his longest continuous employment lasted 18 months.

On February 15, 1933, Sutton and a confederate attempted to rob the Corn Exchange Bank and Trust Company in Philadelphia, Pennsylvania. Sutton, disguised as a mailman, entered the bank early in the morning. The curiosity of a passerby caused the robbery attempt to be abandoned. However, on January 15, 1934 Sutton entered the same bank with two companions through a skylight. When the watchman arrived, they forced him to admit the employees as usual. Each employee was handcuffed and crowded into a small room.

He also pulled a Broadway jewelry store robbery in broad daylight, impersonating a telegraph messenger. Sutton's other disguises included a policeman, messenger and maintenance man.

Sutton acquired two nicknames, "The Actor" and "Slick Willie," for his ingenuity in executing robberies in various disguises.

Fond of expensive clothes, Sutton was described as being an immaculate dresser. Although he was a bank robber, Sutton had the reputation of a gentleman; in fact, people present at his robberies stated he was quite polite. One victim said witnessing one of Sutton's robberies was like being at the movies, except the usher had a gun.

Sutton was apprehended on February 5, 1934, and was sentenced to serve 25 to 50 years in Eastern State Penitentiary in Philadelphia, Pennsylvania, for the machine gun robbery of the Corn Exchange Bank. On April 3, 1945, Sutton was one of 12 convicts who escaped the institution through a tunnel. He was recaptured the same day.

Sentenced to life imprisonment as a four time offender, Sutton was transferred to the Philadelphia County Prison in Homesburg, Pennsylvania. On February 10, 1947, Sutton and other prisoners dressed as prison guards, managed to escape.

On March 20, 1950, Willie "The Actor" Sutton was added to the FBI's list of Ten Most Wanted Fugitives. Because of his love for expensive clothes, Sutton's photograph was given to tailors as well as police departments. A 24-year-old man recognized Sutton on the New York subway on February 18, 1952, and followed him to a local gas station where Sutton purchased a battery for his car. The man reported the incident to the police who later arrested Sutton.

Sutton did not resist his arrest by New York City Police, but denied any robberies or other crimes since his 1947 escape from Philadelphia County Prison. At the time of his arrest, Sutton had one life sentence plus 105 years. He was further sentenced to an additional 30 years to life in New York State Prison.

Seventeen years later, the New York State penal authorities decided that Sutton did not have to serve his complete life sentences. He had emphysema and was preparing for major surgery on his arteries in legs. On December 24, 1969, 68-year-old Sutton was released from Attica State Prison. Ironically, in 1970, Sutton did a television commercial to promote the New Britain Connecticut Bank and Trust Company's new Photo credit card program. On November 2, 1980, Willie Sutton died in Spring Hill, Florida, at the age of 79.

Since Weiser's retirement, he continues to be involved with both Law enforcement and Shomrim. In 1973 he was appointed by then NYPD Police Commissioner Donald F. Cawley to be a consultant for the Department's recruitment program. In this capacity Lou successfully advocated for the establishment of a special police exam which did not take place on Saturdays and so would be available to Jews as well as non-Jews. He was later appointed by President Nixon to the Assay Commission of the United States Mint. He was also appointed by Mayor Rudolph Giuliani to the Civil Service Screening Commission in New York City.

In 2003, Lou was the recipient of the National Shomrim Society Asser Levy Award.

Another 1940 graduate was Al Seedman, who rose to the rank of Chief of Detectives and also served as president of the New York Shomrim Society. Al wrote a best-selling book about his experiences in the police department called *Chief!*

Seedman grew up on Fox Street, near St. Mary's Park, a haven for Irish gangs and one of the toughest neighborhoods in the South Bronx. But he himself didn't have a tough time. "It was a Jewish block," he explained, "and Jewish kids didn't fight." After studying accounting at City College, he joined the department in 1941. "I didn't get the choice assignments," he admitted. "I think it was because I was Jewish. I let it slide off my back." But he did rise through the ranks.

To many people it felt as if Seedman was Chief of Detectives forever, but he served only from 1971 to 1972. He is reported to have been a kind of magnet that kept drawing publicity to himself; there were articles about him everywhere. He was always out in the field, always talking to the press, in part because he had become the department spokesman for what he called "front-page crimes."

In 1972, Alexanders hired Chief Seedman away as vice president in charge of security for all its 15 stores. But even after he left, the myth surrounding him endured. Young Jewish cops used to come up to him and thank him: "They joined the force after reading about me in the papers." He was the Jewish Goliath who seemed to stride over an Irish army. Both Lou and Al were also instrumental in the formation of the National Shomrim and remain proud members of Shomrim to this day (A. Seedman personal communication, 2005).

Another Shomrim legend is Elson Gelfand, a retired Deputy Chief who says that when he joined the department in the 1950's, "there was not a single Jewish policeman above the rank of captain." The Shomrim Society has been a sanctuary for Jewish officers since it was founded. "It was something to identify with so I wouldn't get lost among all the Irish and Italians," said Chief Gelfand, who was its president in 1984. "Otherwise I would have been adrift." Gelfand is irritated that the term "Shomrim cop" has at times had a negative connotation as meaning someone with a soft, cushy desk job. He states that this is not true but was the perception among many officers. But this is one of the reasons Jewish officers needed someone like Al Seedman, a man of action who hated to sit behind a desk (E. Gelfand personal communication, 2005).

On August 11, 1937, three Philadelphia patrolmen, Robert Sharp, Herman Levin and Samuel K. Glass, were detailed at an A&P warehouse strike. Officer Levin brought up the subject of a Philadelphia Jewish police organization based on the NYPD Shomrim Society. The other two officers were enthusiastic about the idea, and on October 26, 1937, a meeting was held with Mayor S. Davis Wilson and Director of Public Safety, Andrew J. Emmanuel, and their official approval was obtained. On November 3, 1937, a contingent of men went to New York and obtained information and ideas for organizing a Shomrim society in Philadelphia from the New York Shomrim Society and the Ner Tamid Society, which was the Jewish firefighter organization.

On November 9, 1937 an organizational meeting was held at Rodeph Shalom Synagogue. Robert Sharp was appointed Chairman of the organization committee. Word was sent to all Jewish members of the Department of Public Safety that a Jewish police and firefighter organization was being formed which also included civilian employees of the Department of Public Safety.

On January 5, 1938, at a meeting at the Beth Israel temple, the name of "Shomrim of Philadelphia" was adopted by the membership. The YMHA (Young Men's Hebrew Association) was selected as a meeting place with meetings to be held on the first Thursday of every month. The main purpose for the establishment of the "Shomrim of Philadelphia" was to create a spirit of fellowship, "So that police, fire, and public safety officers of the Jewish faith may join together for the welfare of all". On January 1, 2000, the name was changed to "Shomrim of Philadelphia and the Delaware Valley" reflecting the growing geographic area being served.

There are now Shomrim Societies all over the country. The Shomrim of Southern California was formed in June, 1982 as the "Los Angeles County Shomrim Association." The organization eventually grew to include members of the law enforcement, public safety, and administration of justice community in all of Southern California. The Society is called a fraternal and social organization formed "to promote the spirit of friendship of its members and their families, to encourage good

fellowship among members, and to advance the welfare of its members."
The Society presently comprises Jewish men and women who support
the welfare of the general community and strive to improve the public
image of the members of all law enforcement, public safety and administration of justice agencies everywhere. It is an affiliate member of
the National Conference of Shomrim Societies.

The South Florida chapter of Shomrim was founded in 1984. A recent
Society president, Robert Singer, a Metro-Dade homicide detective,
stated that Shomrim does much more than battle anti-Semitism. It is
a group in the Jewish community bound together by the common voca-
tion of law enforcement to help the community at large. As a minority
organization there is a special sensitivity to minority concerns of discrimination and harassment no matter what the race or religion. Also,
Shomrim offers more tangible services to the community, such as
sending members to condominiums to instruct elderly residents on
safety, and by raising money and food for needy families.

Among the south Florida society's 125 members, there are two police
chiefs, several judges, prosecutors, probation officers, police officers,
and rabbis serving as police chaplains.

Sources

American Jewish Archives. 2005. Three Hundred and Fifty Years of American Jewry. http://AmericanJewishArchives.org (acquired February 26, 2005).

Costello, Augustine. 2005. Our Police Protectors, History of the New York Police. http://Usgennet.org (acquired February 5, 2005).

Gelfand, Elson. 2006. Personal Communication (January 10, 2006).

Jewish Encyclopedia. 2005. History, Biography, and Sociology. http://Jewishencyclopedia.com (acquired February 26, 2005).

NYPD Shomrim History. 2005. http://Shomrim.org (acquired February 5, 2005).

Seedman, Albert. 2005. *Personal Communication* (November 12, 2005).

Shomrim History. 2005. http://Shomrimpadv.org (acquired November 27, 2005).

chapter 2
Should a Jew be a Cop?

Before looking at whether a Jew should be a cop, we must first decide "who is a Jew." Jews (Hebrew: Yehudim) are followers of Judaism. Jews are also members of the Jewish people (also known as the Jewish nation). Jews are also regarded as an ethno-religious group descended from the ancient Israelites and converts who joined the religion at various times and locations throughout human history. Jews may or may not be religiously observant.

Modern-day orthodox religious Jews regard someone as being Jewish if he or she is a child of a Jewish mother. This is matrilineal transmission of Jewishness. Pure faith-based Judaism sees a person as Jewish if he or she believes in the one God of the Torah, and if not born Jewish, has undergone a proper Jewish conversion. This view is predominant among American Jewry. A cultural Jew is regarded as a person who usually has at least one Jewish parent or grandparent, and who may or may not practice some of the traditional Jewish customs. For the purposes of this book, a member of any of these Jewish groups (i.e., ancestral and matrilineal, faith-based, and cultural), who is a member of law enforcement, is a "Jew in Blue."

The concept of the law, its enforcement, and its adjudication, have always been vital and central percepts of the Jewish religion. In the process of collecting and codifying Israeli law, the great law-giver himself, Moses, had ample precedent. He himself had been brought up at court and was literate. To set down the law in writing, to have it carved in stone, was part of the liberating act of fleeing from Egypt (where there was no statutory law.)

From the fifth to the eleventh centuries BCE, Jewish communities spread throughout the Near East and Mediterranean, and eventually through most of central and eastern Europe. During this time they settled most of their legal problems through religious courts. Seen in western terms, it was natural law, the law of the Bible, the code of Justinian, the canon law, the English common law, the European civil law, the parliamentary statutes, the American Constitution, and the Napoleonic Code all rolled into one. In fact, there has been no other system in the history of the world which has sought for so long to combine moral and ethical teaching with the practical exercise of civil and criminal jurisprudence.

In his book *A History of the Jews*, Paul Johnson provides some of the rationale for the Biblical intertwining of criminal and religious law.

> If indeed God owns everything and everyone, He is an injured party in all offenses of man against his fellow men. A sin against God is serious but a sin against a fellow man is more serious since it is against God too. Indeed, God is the "Invisible Third" in all interactions between men. Hence, if God is the only witness to a transaction, false denial of it is worse than if there is a written transaction. Robbery is not as bad as secret theft since he who commits the latter shows he has more respect for the earthly power of man than the divine vengeance of God (p. 157).

For Jews, man has always been regarded both as an individual with concomitant rights, and as a member of a community with associated responsibilities and obligations. Just as the individual man benefited from the worth of his community, so he was obliged to contribute to it. Not the least of these obligations is obedience to the community's duly constituted authorities. Such authorities have traditionally constructed various bye-laws, and also had powers to punish offenders.

Implicit in the Hebrew Bible is the holistic notion that one man's sin, however small, affects the whole community, indeed the entire world, if even imperceptibly. In the same vein, a wise man must give of his wisdom to the community, just as a rich man must give of his wealth. So it is a sin not to serve when required.

What is an appropriate profession for a Jew? The Talmud seems to prefer occupations that involve helping others and which contribute to the welfare of society (Babylonian Talmud, Sanhedrin 24b-25a). An occupation should be productive and make a person responsible and honest.

Oleynu is one of the oldest of Jewish prayers (some claim that it goes back to the time of Joshua making it more than 3,000 years ago). One phrase in this prayer deals with *tikkun olam*, and describes the ideal society "when the world will be perfected under the reign of the Almighty." The concept of *tikkun olam* includes alleviating such world problems as poverty, racism, pollution, and oppression. The sages of the Talmud used the principle of *tikkun olam* to legislate various laws, amendments, and enactments to help society and to prevent conflicts.

Professions that improve the world are certainly admirable. *Tikkun olam* is a major part of the cabala of the great Rabbi Isaac Luria. In fact, Rabbi Luria once remarked that the reason for so much of the world's problems such as hunger, hatred and war was because God needs mankind's "help" in repairing the world.

But the Talmud does not seem to prefer occupations which involve authority over others. Shemaya stated (Babylonian Talmud, Avot 1:10):

"Love work, hate being in a position of authority, and do not become overly intimate with the ruling authorities." Shemaya felt that people in positions of authority are arrogant, pompous, and overbearing.

It is unlikely that any one profession could possess (or avoid) all of these characteristics. But all in all, the Talmud suggests that a good profession (1) provides an individual with time for spiritual pursuits; (2) does not tempt one to become dishonest or sexually immoral; (3) allows one to help people and society; (4) is profitable and enables one to become wealthy; and (5) is clean, pleasant, and dignified.

So is police work a good profession for a Jew? The hours can be terribly long, the temptation for dishonesty can be monumental, it is not profitable or wealth-inducing, and it can be extremely unpleasant and even horrific. So by Talmudic standards police work may not be a good profession for a Jew.

What about knowledge and education? A remarkable aspect of the Jewish people which helps explain why Jews have survived as a people is the pursuit of learning. Through the ages and up until modern times, Jews were the only people on Earth that were literate as an entire people. This universal literacy together with a common language seems to have bound Jewish communities together wherever in the world they went. Literacy engendered knowledge, and enabled Jews to transmit knowledge to other Jews everywhere. Literacy and learning were always revered as essential to Judaism, and accounted for Jews becoming prominent among the professions that required literacy, such as science, medicine, and law. These disciplines were of basic value to the development of the societies in which Jews have been immersed.

Arthur Niederhoffer was a lawyer, sociologist, NYPD lieutenant, and a Jew. He discussed why police work might be the <u>wrong</u> career for a Jew, a difficult life, and even a source of embarrassment, in his 1967 book, *Behind the Shield*. A Jewish policeman in New York City (at least in the 1960s) according to Niederhoffer, was always trying to "prove himself" to the classically Irish police force who would never trust that a Jew would want to be a cop. Many Jewish officers faced what Niederhoffer termed "anti-intellectualism" in that non-Jews on the police department would view with extreme distrust and even contempt the Jewish officer's attempts to actually "solve problems" on the street using "persuasion" and "verbal skills" rather than brute force (Neiderhoffer, 1967).

From the 1940s to at least the 1970s (and perhaps continuing today) Jewish police officers have been symbolic of the trend towards greater professionalism and formal education in police agencies across the country. But according to Niederhoffer, this created additional problems for Jewish officers as the old-timers resented what they saw as favoritism towards these college-educated new officers.

For Niederhoffer, the emergence of college-educated Jewish police officers fostered alienation in police departments because these officers had a wider "cosmopolitan" view of their work in contrast to the narrow, tried-and-true police traditions which have prevailed in these agencies.

Niederhoffer described certain recurrent and unpleasant situations that confronted Jewish policemen. One of these was when the non-Jewish policeman tried to be friendly with the Jewish officer by greeting him with "*Mach a leben?*" To the non-Jew this is equivalent to asking, "How are things?" To the Jew it was (aside from bad grammar), an inference that Jews are mainly concerned with making money (p. 76).

Niederhoffer recounted how in the 1940s, 50s, and 60s it was indeed a source of Jewish embarrassment to be a policeman. He describes how Jewish mothers-in-law had learned subtle techniques to disguise their disappointment at having gained a policeman for a son-in-law. For example, a mother-in-law might introduce her policeman son-in-law as a "college graduate with two degrees." Others would try to conceal the police blemish by describing the policeman relative as being involved "in youth work" or as "a teacher." Many Jewish parents would suspect other Jews of translating the words "My son, the cop" into another altogether different phrase "My cop-son." In Yiddish colloquial speech the term of mild contempt commonly used to signify "a person who will never amount to anything" is pronounced phonetically as "cop son" (Neiderhoffer, 1967).

Another problem with being a Jewish police officer, according to Niederhoffer, was the proclivity of developing a sense of cynicism which can be disabling at times. He found that most police officers (Jew and non-Jew) were cynical of the world around them, and that this became more chronic and deeply rooted the longer they remained on the force where they faced daily disillusionment and corruption of idealism. It was likely to be worse if the officer was not promoted, did not get choice assignments, or did not receive recognition from other officers as well as superiors.

For Jewish officers, this cynicism was the heaviest since the Jewish tradition stresses that success in life lies in becoming a professional person. A Jewish police officer who remains at a low rank is thus a "double failure," in that he did not become a doctor or a lawyer, and he has been unable to rise up the ranks within the police department.

Dr. Stephen M. Passamaneck, in his scholarly treatise on *Police Ethics and the Jewish Tradition,* presents further reasons why law enforcement is not generally considered to be a proper career for Jewish men and women. He cites the fear and suspicion that Jews have felt as part of their "Jewish immigrant mindset" as being paramount in this (Passamaneck, 2003).

It is known, for example, of the horrors that Jews had to endure during the Pogroms of Czarist Russia and similar tortures in central Europe, where the police acted as the agents of anti-Jewish governments. In addition, during the nineteenth and twentieth centuries when Jews immigrated in large numbers to western countries (including the United States), police departments did not exactly open their arms to the "huddled Jewish masses" as Emma Lazarus, herself a Jew, might have wished.

Nevertheless, Biblical history does indicate that Jews have always been involved in some sort of police work. The modern Hebrew word for police office is shoter (plural shotrim). This term appears in *Deuteronomy*, the *Book of Joshua*, and the *Books of Chronicles*. The *Tosefta* notes that shotrims are officers of the judges used to enforce judicial orders. Moses Mainonides (1135-1204) mentions shotrim as the armed judicial police who patrol public areas such as marketplaces, shops, and gardens. In particular, such shotrim were described as being utilized during festival times where men and women might gather in order to prevent any "overindulgence" which could lead to [sexual] transgressions.

In the time of Moses shotrim referred to the elders who shared the high tasks of governance and justice in the community. Prior to the destruction of the Second Temple in 70 CE, the shotrim had the duty of temple administration and protection.

Biblical tradition defines the qualities necessary for a person to be a shotrim. These included the highest degree of ethical principles and moral character, and the ability to make sound decisions which potentially affect the lives and property of many people.

So it seems that although police work may not seem like an ideal profession for a Jew, Jews have been doing it for at least four thousand years.

Sources

Baron, S. (1953). *A Social and Religious History of the Jews*. New York: Columbia University Press.

Eckstein, Z. (1998). *Ideal Occupations: The Talmudic Perspective*. Eitan Berglas School of Economics.

Johnson, P. (1987). *A History of the Jews*. New York: Harper and Row.

Niederhoffer, A, (1967) *Behind the Shield*. New York: Doubleday and Company.

Passamaneck, S. (2003). *Police Ethics and the Jewish Tradition*. New York: CC Thomas.

Chapter 3
Feds

Reuben Etting

The first known Jew in the state of Maryland arrived in the 1640's. His name was Jacob Lumbrozo. But it was not until the mid-18th century that Jews began to establish themselves as family units in Maryland, settling primarily in the mercantile community of Baltimore. By the time of the American revolution, they were integral members of the business community, and over the next century Baltimore was to become a major center of Jewish life in America. Reuben Etting, a major supporter of President Thomas Jefferson, was appointed by Jefferson as the U.S. Marshall for Maryland in 1801.

Etting was the first Jew ever to be appointed to a major U.S. governmental position. Yet Etting could not even be elected dog catcher in his own State of Maryland because of the "test oath requirements" imposed by the state. Under these restrictive requirements, a Maryland elected official had to swear "upon his faith as a Christian" that he would uphold the laws of the State of Maryland. A Jew making that declaration would be lying and so was automatically excluded from holding office. For a Jew to hold elected office in Maryland, that state's constitution would have to be changed.

Seventeen years after Etting's appointment, a Scotch Presbyterian immigrant named Thomas Kennedy was elected to the Maryland House of Delegates from Western Maryland. Kennedy, an ardent believer in Jeffersonian Republicanism, had never known, or for that matter had never met, a Jew in his life. In the State legislature in Annapolis Maryland, he learned of the political denial of rights to Jews. He recognized that a denial of rights to one group was a denial of rights to all. Accordingly, and due primarily to his efforts, the state constitution was eventually changed and the test oath requirements were eliminated.

The struggle for a Jew to be able to hold office was shown extreme acrimony in the state of Maryland to be sure, but it was no less a struggle in other States. As late as 1824, Massachusetts refused to do away with its own Christian test oath rather than give Jews the right to hold elected office. Former president John Adams himself was unsuccessful in his attempts to change the law.

North Carolina was the last hold out for a Protestant religious test oath. It was not until the reconstruction era in 1868 before the government of North Carolina changed the constitution to allow Jews to hold office. That same year, the first Jewish Congregation in North Carolina was legally organized and received its State Charter for legal existence. The Jewish community of Wilmington built the first permanent Jewish house of worship in North Carolina, the Temple of Israel, in July 1876.

It was not until 1845 that the first person of Jewish background was elected to the United States Congress. But in order for David Yulee to be elected, he had to abandon his Jewish roots, change his name from Levy and convert to Christianity. Yulee County, Florida is named after him. The first individual who actually maintained his Jewish identity to be elected to the U.S. Congress was Judah P. Benjamin from Louisiana. Benjamin would later become the Secretary of War and then the Secretary of State of the Confederate States of America during the Civil War.

President James Madison appointed the nation's first Jewish Ambassador ever, Mordechai Emanuel Noah, as American Counsel to Tunisia in 1813. But Noah was recalled when the Muslim government of Tunisia learned he was a Jew. For Jews in federal law enforcement, not much happened for the next 150 years.

Edward H. Levi

Edward H. Levi took the oath of office on February 7, 1975 to become the nation's 71st Attorney General and the only Jew (to this day) to hold that office. He was sworn in at a Department of Justice Ceremony attended by President Ford and Vice President Rockefeller. The oath was administered by Associate Supreme Court Justice Lewis F. Powell, Jr.

In President Ford's cabinet, Levi served with such other luminaries as Henry Kissinger (Secretary of State), William Simon (Secretary of the Treasure), Elliot Richardson (Secretary of Commerce), Donald Rumsfeld (Secretary of Defense), and Casper Weinberger (Secretary of Health, Education, and Welfare).

Edward Hirsch Levi was born in Chicago on June 26, 1911, to Gerson B. Levi, a rabbi who came to the United States from Scotland, and Elsa Hirsch Levi. His maternal grandfather, Rabbi Emil G. Hirsch, was an early member of the University of Chicago faculty and a leading architect of the Reform branch of Judaism in America.

After graduating from college, Mr. Levi began studying for a doctorate in literature at the university of Chicago, but dropped out after being told in a friendly manner by a professor, that he would never be given a position in the humanities department at Chicago or any leading institution because he was a Jew.

He recalled that incident not ruefully but joyfully in an essay in *Newsweek* magazine during the time of the nation's bicentennial celebrations of 1976 to demonstrate how much the country had changed. He had, after all, become the first Jewish dean of a major law school. When he became the president of the University of Chicago in 1968, he said he believed he was the first Jewish president of a major private university other than one with a clear Jewish identity, like Brandeis.

During World War II, Levi served as special assistant to U.S. Attorney General Francis Biddle and as first assistant in the Antitrust Division under Assistant Attorney General Thurman Arnold. In 1945, he returned to the University of Chicago as Professor of Law and was appointed Dean of the Law School in 1950. Upon his death in 2000, The University of Chicago News Office quoted Supreme Court Justice John Paul Stevens, a colleague of Levi on the University of Chicago faculty, "I would add that his contributions to the nation during his service as its attorney general, when recovery from the trauma of Watergate required a firm hand and sound judgment at the top of the legal profession, were of the same matchless quality and perhaps of even greater importance in restoring trust in our government" (March 2000, p. 5).

Former President Ford said:

> Ed Levi was a superb attorney general. In the early 1970s,
> the Nixon Department of Justice was in great difficulty because
> of Watergate and the tragedy of the Vietnam War. The Amer-
> ican people and the Congress had lost respect because of
> ineffective and inappropriate leadership. When I assumed the
> presidency in August 1974, it was essential that a new attor-
> ney general be appointed who would restore integrity and
> competence to the Department of Justice . . . In retrospect, as
> president, I am proud to say Ed Levi was one of my finest
> cabinet members. I thank him for his outstanding service as
> attorney general at a very critical time in America's history
> (March 2000, p. 2).

Under Levi, both the Justice Department and the FBI had to deal
with organized crime on a continual basis. Since the late 19th century,
these groups of organized criminals in which most members were of
Italian background, had been among the most active and powerful in
this country. While these groups were called by various names—the
Black Hand, the Mafia, the Organization, the mob, organized crime—
collectively they were known as La Cosa Nostra. Their origins can
be traced back to southern Italy, where in certain areas particularly
Sicily, Calabria, and Naples, where secret criminal societies had
emerged centuries ago. In general, all these groups concentrated on
extortion, bootlegging, protection rackets, and a category of crimes
called by some as victimless—gambling, prostitution, narcotics, and
loansharking. To insure success in its criminal enterprises, these organized crime groups engaged in systematic attempts to corrupt and
bribe law enforcement officers, members of the judicial system, and
political leaders. Most typically, this took the form of bribes, favors,
campaign contributions, and help in getting out the vote. Where the
machinery of a political party could be controlled, organized crime
ran its own candidates at all levels—local to federal.

In order to fight an effective battle against organized crime, the FBI had to use many methods of gathering intelligence, including wire-tapping and electronic surveillance. The use of these techniques were seen as valid when investigating criminals. However, when the FBI began using these methods to investigate non-criminal Americans seen as "subversive" or as holding extreme political views, the story was different. But this was exactly the situation in which Levi found himself during the mid-1970s.

The Federal Bureau of Investigation had been conducting domestic surveillance operations that were probably unconstitutional. Mr. Levi forced through regulations setting limits on what the bureau and the Central Intelligence Agency could undertake while conducting investigations and gathering intelligence.

The FBI had been using "counter-subversive" surveillance techniques and kept lists of people and groups judged to be potential national security threats since the days of the Red Scare in the 1920s. Such activities were expanded in the late 1930s when Franklin Roosevelt instructed the FBI to gather information about Fascist and Communist activities in the US and to conduct investigations into possible espionage and sabotage.

FBI director J. Edgar Hoover interpreted these directives as authorizing open-ended and ongoing inquiries into the lives and activities of all those American who he considered to be "potential subversives."

Hoover apparently repeatedly misinformed a succession of indifferent presidents and attorneys general about the precise scope of Roosevelt's original directives, and managed for more than 30 years to elicit tacit executive approval for continuous FBI investigations into a never-ending and expanding class of political, and possible political dissidents.

The beginning of the Cold War, ongoing conflicts with the Soviet Union, and America's fears of an international Communist conspiracy, provided all the justification the CIA needed for world-wide covert operations, but it also contributed to the FBI's rationale for expanding its domestic surveillance activities.

In 1957, without Congressional or presidential authorization, Hoover launched a highly secret operation called "COINTELPRO." For the next 17 years, the FBI began investigations on more than half a million 'subversive' Americans using techniques such as wire-tapping, bugging, mail-openings, and break-ins. The bureau also utilized informers and undercover operatives to infiltrate and report on the activities and membership of political associations ranging from the Socialist Workers Party to the NAACP to the Medical Committee for Human Rights to a Milwaukee Boy Scout troop.

In addition to investigation and surveillance, COINTELPRO was to discredit, weaken, and ultimately destroy the New Left and Black radical movements of the sixties and early seventies, i.e., to silence the major sources of political dissent and opposition. One of the groups in the FBI's sights was Students for a Democratic Society. Students for a Democratic Society (SDS), was a radical student organization founded in 1960 which called for students to join in a movement to establish "participatory democracy."

The SDS developed from the youth branch of a socialist educational organization known as the League for Industrial Democracy (LID) which descended from the Intercollegiate Socialist Society which was started in 1905. SDS held its first meeting in 1960 at Ann Arbor, Michigan, where Robert Alan Haber was elected president.

The political manifesto of SDS, known as the Port Huron Statement, criticized the political system of the United States for failing to achieve international peace and failing to address social ills in contemporary society. It also advocated non-violent civil disobedience as the means by which student youth could bring forth their participatory democracy.

In the academic year 1962-63 the President of SDS was Tom Hayden. There were nine chapters with, at most, about 1000 members. By 1964 the organization had grown substantially and also became more violent. On October 1, 1964, the University of California Berkeley exploded into one of the SDS's first acts of civil disobedience. Led by a charismatic student activist named Mario Savio, upwards of three thousand students surrounded a police car in which a student arrested for setting up a card table in defiance of a ban by the University was being taken away. The sit-down prevented the police car from moving for over 36 hours. The demonstrations, meetings and strikes that were to follow all but shut the University down and hundreds of students were arrested.

In February of 1965 Lyndon Johnson dramatically escalated the war in Vietnam by bombing North Vietnam and increasing the number of ground troops involved in directly fighting the Viet Cong in the South. The draft became a very real factor in the lives of the students on American campuses. Chapters of SDS all over the country started to lead small, localized demonstrations against the war, and the first "teach-in" against the war was held in the University of Michigan. Soon hundreds more, all over the country were held. SDS became the leading student group against the Vietnam war on most U.S. campuses.

By the Fall of 1966 there were on the order of 175 active SDS chapters, and about 6000 members. Chants of "Hell no,we won't go!" were being heard on college campuses all over the country along with the first public burnings of draft-cards. In the Spring of 1968, SDS led an effort on the campuses called "Ten Days of Resistance" and local chapters cooperated with the Student Mobilization Committee in rallies, marches, sit-ins and teach-ins, which culminated in a one day strike on April 26. About a million students stayed away from classes that day—the largest ever in the history of the country.

Another group of immense interest to the FBI was the Black Planters. "The Black Panther Party for Self-Defense" as they were originally called, was formed in Oakland, California in October, 1966 by Huey P. Newton and Bobby Seale. Later the name of the party was changed simply to Black Panther Party.

The party was formed to fight what was seen as the blatant racism prevailing in the United States. The Panthers were well versed with self-defense tactics and many of them were fully armed. Law Enforcement agencies were quick to put down any resistance and many shoot outs took place in those neighborhoods where the Panthers had offices and large memberships.

The FBI also used agent provocateurs to destroy the credibility of leaders by framing them, bringing false charges against them, distributing offensive materials published in their name, spreading false rumors, sabotaging equipment, stealing money, and other dirty tricks.

Government documents showed that the FBI was involved in creating acrimonious disputes within SDS and the Black Panthers, which eventually led to their break-up. In order to discredit various radicals, they were portrayed as criminals, adulterers, or government agents.

These activities finally came to public attention because of the Watergate investigations, congressional hearings, and information obtained under the Freedom of Information Act (FOIA). It was in response to these kinds of revelations that led Attorney General Levi to initiate the public guidelines governing the initiation and scope of the FBI's domestic security investigations.

The United States Senate's Select Committee to Study Governmental Operations with Respect to Intelligence Activities, issued the results of its own investigation into the government's internal intelligence-gathering activities. The Committee's findings supported those of the Attorney General as well as his initiatives. The Committee felt the matter important enough to declare:

> Free government depends upon the ability of all its citizens to speak their minds without fear of official sanction. The ability of ordinary people to be heard by their leaders means that they must be free to join in groups in order more effectively to express their grievances. Constitutional safeguards are needed to protect the timid as well as the courageous, the weak as well as the strong. While many Americans have been willing to assert their beliefs in the face of possible governmental reprisals, no citizen should have to weigh his or her desire to express an opinion, or join a group, against the risk of having lawful speech or association used against him.

We do not believe the Executive has, or should have, the inherent constitutional authority to violate the law or infringe the legal rights of Americans, whether it be a warrantless break-in into the home or office of an American, warrantless electronic surveillance, or a President's authorization to the FBI to create a massive domestic security program based upon secret oral directives (1976, book II).

Although he was appointed by a Republican president, Levi's performance was considered so nonpartisan that when he left the Justice Department to return to the University of Chicago, he was warmly praised by Senator Edward M. Kennedy, Democrat of Massachusetts.

In a speech in the Senate, Kennedy said, "Mr. Levi entered office under the most difficult and trying circumstances, yet he leaves a department once again characterized by integrity, intellectual honesty and commitment to equal justice" (January 25, 1977).

Bonnie Gail Tischler

Bonnie Gail Tischler was born in New York and grew up in Florida. After receiving a degree in broadcast communications from the University of Florida in 1966, she worked for a while in New York before moving to Washington. She eventually took a position as an Equal Employment Opportunity investigator, and helped to organize the Interagency Committee on Women in Law Enforcement.

In the *U.S. Customs TODAY* magazine, Tischler recalled how in 1971, when President Nixon signed the executive order granting women equal status in the federal law enforcement community, a few pioneering women were needed to take the first steps and eventually to break the glass ceiling. Tischler helped do that.

She learned about the sky marshal program from her roommates who were flight attendants and shortly thereafter become one of the first female United States sky marshals. She remembers her parents being shocked at her decision. After all, she later recalled, "My mother always said that nice Jewish girls don't go into law enforcement" (June 2000).

Tischler recalls that back in 1971, when women started out in the federal sector in law enforcement positions, there were so many apocryphal stories about how a male agent could possibly be out on surveillance with a female. "People would question whether or not [a male agent] was actually watching the event or messing around with the 'girl' . . . you know, could a woman actually handle a gun, would she back you up in terms of a raid or some other enforcement activity?" (June 2000)

Tischler became a special agent with the U.S. Customs Service in 1977. She would later confide that she knew she was joining what she called "a guy kind of environment" but subsequently "fell in love with law enforcement."

The U.S. Customs Service is charged with protecting the borders of the United States from dangerous cargo or persons either entering or leaving the country. "It's a soup to nuts agency," said Ms. Tischler since the agency enforces Customs laws as well as laws pertaining to the Food and Drug Administration, Department of Agriculture, the Drug Enforcement Administration, and others.

In 1980, she became the only female agent assigned to Operation Greenback, a newly formed task force in Miami that pioneered the investigative technique of tracking illicit money back to drug kingpins.

Tischler excelled in this role and was known as "the girl with the golden gun" for the small, gold-plated Smith & Wesson .38 she carried in her handbag. She bought the golden gun when she was investigating Colombian drug traffickers, who favored flashy clothes and ostentatious gold jewelry. The golden gun was such a success that drug traffickers regularly offered to buy it from her even as she was arrested them.

Considered a financial whiz, Tischler was eventually transferred back to Washington in 1983 to supervise the agency's financial operations. In 1986, she became director of the Smuggling Investigations Division and helped integrate the agency's tactical operations with narcotics, financial, child pornography and general smuggling investigations. She also headed the agency's marine branch and would later say in an interview with The Center for Business of Government: "What do I know about boats? I don't do boats. I do Bloomingdale's." Despite her misgivings, she studied the technical manuals for the vessels under her command and soon learned to operate them (December 18, 2000).

In 1987, she became special agent in charge of North Florida, based in Tampa, where she supervised agents investigating money laundering at the Bank of Credit and Commerce International. The bank became the target in one of the largest money-laundering cases ever prosecuted. In 1995, she became special agent in charge of South Florida, which was the largest investigative unit within the Customs Service.

In 1997, Tischler became the first female Assistant Commissioner for the office of investigations of the Customs Service, and in 2000 she became the agency's first woman to serve as Assistant Commissioner for field operations. In this capacity, she had responsibility for all cargo and passenger processing in the United States as well as the investigations of air and marine interdiction operations, communications, and intelligence activities of more than 4,500 enforcement personnel.

Tischler was always especially interested in those tasks and cases which had national security and anti-terrorism implications. For example, in 1996 and 1997 the U.S. Customs Service had been investigating the dealings between IBM East Europe/Asia Ltd. (the Russian subsidiary of International Business Machines), and a Russian nuclear weapons laboratory. In July 1998 IBM pled guilty to illegally exporting computers to the laboratory (called "Arzamas-16") and received the maximum criminal fine of $8.5 million plus the maximum civil fine of $171,000. IBM admitted to selling and exporting the computers while having reason to believe that the computers would be used directly or indirectly in the research, development, design, manufacture, construction, testing, or maintenance of nuclear devices.

Tischler, together with the United States Attorney's office, noted that these unlawful transactions constituted serious violations of export laws designed to protect the national security of the United States and further this country's non-proliferation goals. They further noted that IBM cooperated with the government's investigation and acted in a responsible manner in bringing resolution to the case.

Tischler was clearly a leader. She discussed the essential qualities of leadership with The Center for Business of Government, citing that the most important component is credibility. "I really think that everything spins off credibility . . . I believe in participatory management . . . it doesn't matter to me whether I'm popular or not with the troops . . . but it does matter to me if I have their respect and that they follow what I ask them to do because they believe in me and they believe in the mission" (December 18, 2000).

She was fond of relating a story about when she first came into headquarters taking over a smuggling division called "Tactful Enforcement." One of the patrol officers who was retired military, came to her and said, "I want you to know ma'am, you have my undying loyalty." She recalls thinking at the time, "You just cannot fork over loyalty . . . but you can immediately fork over respect, and I think that's what everybody expects . . . but loyalty is something that you have to earn, and you can only earn that if you're a credible manager" (December 18, 2000).

Since 1972, women have been in a number of situations that have proven the fact that they can handle the job just as well as their male counterparts. "I think it's real important to touch the bases and ring the bells," stated Tischler. "I think it's important to our male counterparts. I think it's important to the women. I think that it's a credibility issue. I think you can't become a manager unless you've done the job, and the people who think they can skip the rungs of the ladder are sadly mistaken."

For Tischler, the "glass ceiling doesn't exist anymore." Women are first-line supervisors, they are second-line management, they are executives, they are serving as "SACs" or "special agents in charge" in all federal law enforcement agencies. But she admits that certain things have not changed. "Mostly, if I'm at a meeting, it's 99.9

percent male. All in the same gray, and black, and dark-blue suits. It's a real treat when there happens to be a woman, either in another agency or somebody who's a peer at one of these meetings," she states (December 18, 2000).

Tischler's role models have been men, and she followed their lead in command and control activities. But when she tried to do some of the things that the "fellows" were doing, such as going out for drinks or using colorful language, it didn't work for her. She rationalized by thinking ". . . I don't have to be like them, I just have to be myself."

Tischler considered retiring in 2001 but stayed on after the September 11 terrorist attacks to work on the twin tasks of keeping trade and the economy moving while enhancing border security. After retiring from government service in 2002, she became a product vice president in the Arlington Virginia office of Pinkerton Global Transportation. She held that position until her untimely death in 2005.

Roslynn R. Mauskopf

On September 3, 2002 Roslynn R. Mauskopf was appointed the United States Attorney for the Eastern District of New York. In this capacity, she is responsible for overseeing all federal criminal and civil cases in Brooklyn, Queens and Staten Island, as well as Nassau and Suffolk Counties. She supervises a staff of approximately 180 attorneys and over 140 support personnel.

From October 6, 1995 to August 30, 2002, Ms. Mauskopf served as New York State Inspector General, appointed by Governor George E. Pataki. She directed the statewide, independent office responsible for investigating allegations of corruption, fraud, criminal activity, conflicts of interest, and abuse in Executive Branch agencies.

Under her leadership, teams of investigators and attorneys worked proactively, often with state, local and federal law enforcement agencies and prosecutors, on thousands of complaints involving bribery, theft, procurement fraud, narcotics, excessive use of force, ethics violations, and other forms of corruption. Cases have resulted in criminal

prosecution, disciplinary action, ethics sanctions, and recommenda-
tions for systemic reform that have improved the efficiency and
accountability of state agencies.

On January 23, 1999, Governor Pataki appointed Inspector General
Mauskopf as Chair of the Governor's Moreland Act Commission on
New York City Schools, charged with examining the operations and
fiscal affairs of the New York City Board of Education and the New
York City School Construction Authority.

The Commission uncovered systemic abuses in the manner in which
the Board reported student attendance and enrollment by including
on active student rosters children that had died, moved out of the city
or country, attended private or parochial school, or were chronic truants.
With respect to school construction, the Commission focused on mis-
management and violations of law in capital planning and construction,
the causes of significant cost overruns and scheduling delays, dilap-
idated facilities, hazardous safety violations, and other issues that
affected the administration of New York City's multi-billion-dollar
capital construction program.

From 1982 to 1995, Ms. Mauskopf served as an Assistant District
Attorney in the New York County District Attorney's Office. She
handled hundreds of violent crimes and white-collar cases, including
the investigation of organized crime's control of trucking in the New
York City garment industry, and the largest theft of client funds by
an attorney in U.S. history.

Mauskopf was named Deputy Chief of the Special Prosecutions
Bureau in 1992 where she supervised and trained prosecutors on financial crimes, investigative techniques, grand jury practice and trial skills.
In 1993, she became Chief of the Frauds Bureau, leading the investigation and prosecution of complex white-collar offenses including
bank, insurance and securities fraud, political corruption, organized
crime, tax fraud, and cybercrime.

As United States Attorney, Mauskopf must deal with issues affecting terrorism on a daily basis and she is a supporter of the Patriot
Act. "In addition to bullets and bombs, money is the lifeblood of ter-

rorists. And, in the Eastern district of New York, we have used the Patriot Act and many of its provisions to choke off the supply of money to terrorists." As an example, is a case prosecuted in the Eastern District of New York, were Mouskopf used the Patriot Act to secure convictions of Mohammed Al-Moayad and Mohammed Zayed (Mauskopf, 2004).

Both of these individuals were Yemeni citizens. Mohammed Al-Moayad was the self-proclaimed spiritual adviser to Osama bin Laden. Using the provisions of the Patriot Act, Mouskopf was able to convict these two individuals of material support of terrorism, for funneling over $20 million to Al Qaeda and Hamas. They were seeking to raise millions of dollars more in support of terrorism. With the help of the Patriot Act provisions, these two terrorist financiers are now in federal prison, each serving 75 and 45 years respectively. She has stated that without the provisions of the Patriot Act, she would not have been able to build and prove this case against these terrorist financiers.

Mauskopf's office also prosecutes murder, narcotics, and gang-related crimes in her jurisdiction. In 2003, she, along with the Richmond County District Attorney, the Bureau of Alcohol, Tobacco, Firearms & Explosives, and New York City Police Department were able to secure an indictment against five members of a violent criminal enterprise, "the Stapleton Crew," who terrorized the residents of the Stapleton section of Staten Island for years.

The defendants, Ronnel Wilson, also known as "Rated R," Michael Whitten, Paris Bullock, Angel Rodriquez, also known as "ICE," and Jamal Brown, also known as "Mal," were named in a 30-count indictment charging crimes such as racketeering, murder, murder conspiracies, narcotics trafficking, obstruction of justice, carjacking, robbery and firearms offenses.

According to the indictment, the defendants frequently engaged in drive-by shootings on public streets against rival gang members, thus endangering the lives of many innocent bystanders. Crew members were also charged with robbing a taxi driver, conspiring to rob "Oz," a Staten Island commercial clothing store, and terrorizing various

Staten Island neighborhoods with violence and intimidation for years. This violent activity culminated with the alleged execution of two police officers.

Mauskopf has also handled numerous racketeering and organized crime complaints such as one in 1995 filed under the civil provisions of the Racketeer Influenced and Corrupt Organizations Act ("RICO") against the International Longshoreman's Association of the AFL-CIO ("ILA").

The charges were based on decades of evidence relating to corruption and organized crime influence within the union and businesses operating on the New York / New Jersey waterfront and the Port of Miami. For decades the waterfront had been the setting for corruption and violence stemming from organized crime's influence over labor unions operating there, including the ILA and its affiliated locals, as well as port-related businesses.

Since the late 1950's, two organized crime families – the Gambino family and the Genovese family – shared control of various ports, with the Gambino family primarily exercising its influence at commercial shipping terminals in Brooklyn and Staten Island, and the Genovese family primarily controlling those in Manhattan, New Jersey and the Port of Miami.

Mauskopf's office was able to link the leadership of the Genovese and Gambino organized crime families to various top ILA officials. These cases resulted in convictions of more than a dozen high-level mob members (including John Gotti) and associates of these two crime families for their roles in controlling the docks along the Eastern seaboard.

A particularly morally reprehensible and disgusting case was handled by Mauskopf's office in 2005, when two retired NYPD detectives were charged with moonlighting as hit men for the mob and allegedly carrying out at least one gangland execution and aiding in at least seven others.

In what could be the worst scandal in NYPD history, Louis Eppolito, 56, and Stephen Caracappa, 63, were were charged by federal prosecutors with taking part in the murders on behalf of the Mafia even while one or both were still active members of the police department.

The charges were among the most startling allegations of police corruption in memory. In one instance, in 1990, prosecutors said the detectives, driving an unmarked police car, pulled over a Mafia captain on the Belt Parkway in Brooklyn and shot him to death for a rival mob figure. In another, in 1986, they allegedly flashed their badges to kidnap a mobster, then threw him in the trunk of their car and delivered him to a rival mobster who tortured and killed him.

For years, Mauskopf charged, the men had been paid handsomely for their role in mob-ordered killings and for routinely funneling secret information about criminal investigations to other members of organized crime. In most of the killings, she said, they did not pull the trigger but helped other hit men track down the victims, at one point becoming so instrumental that they were put on the mob's payroll at $4,000 a month each.

Mr. Eppolito, 56, once co-wrote a book about his life as a police officer whose relatives were in the mob, and Mr. Caracappa, 63, worked in a police unit that was responsible for investigating mob killings. Mr. Eppolito retired in 1990, Mr. Caracappa two years later.

For more than a decade, the men, while collecting their police pensions, have lived across the street from one another in an affluent gated community in Las Vegas, Mr. Caracappa working as a private investigator and Mr. Eppolito playing bit parts in nearly a dozen popular movies—including *Goodfellas*—portraying mobsters, hoodlums and drug dealers.

The former detectives were charged with a racketeering conspiracy, which includes their roles in killings, two attempted murders, obstruction of justice, money laundering and other crimes. The indictment accused them of working as secret associates of the Luchese crime family. They were also charged with disclosing the identity of six cooperating witnesses - three of whom were killed – and compromising several federal and state investigations.

Both men joined the force in 1969, a year in which the city, with abbreviated background checks, hired an unusual number of officers who were later arrested or fired.

Louis Eppolito and Steve Caracappa could potentially receive sentences for first-degree murder for acts committed while they were police officers. But they would not be the first in New York history. The other famous cop to be convicted of murder – and executed – was one Lieutenant Charles Becker. It just so happens that Becker was unfortunately a Jew in blue.

Charles Becker was born to a family of Jewish-German immigrants in upstate New York. He had worked as a baker's assistant and Bowery beer-garden bouncer prior to joining the police department in 1893. He was married three times. His first wife died of pneumonia (although there were rumors that he had drowned her in the bathtub). His second wife divorced him and married his brother. His third marriage in 1905 was the one that lasted.

Becker was an extremely aggressive officer who apparently had no difficulty making up charges against a person if there were not legitimate ones to pursue. Once he was asked for directions by a respectable New Jersey woman who did not understand his answer and asked him to repeat it, he arrested her as being drunk and disorderly. On another occasion, he and his partner shot at a suspected burglar, killed an innocent bystander, and tried to cover up the events by claiming that the dead bystander was the burglar.

In 1896, on a Manhattan street corner, he arrested and sought to railroad an innocent woman on prostitution charges. He might have gotten away with it had his actions not been witnessed by the woman's companion, Stephen Crane, the famous novelist and author of "The Red Badge of Courage." In the years that followed, there were many other civilian complaints against Becker.

Despite all these examples of Becker's questionable ethics, in 1905 he was selected for a special "shoofly squad" that went on occasional raiding rampages throughout the city, gaining Becker a reputation as someone who would arrest his own grandmother if he thought it would make him look good at headquarters.

In 1911, Police Commissioner Rheinlander Waldo placed Becker in command of a special squad charged with going after gangsters and suppressing the city's gambling under-world. It was, wrote one newspaperman, like "putting the fox in charge of the chicken coop." He wasted no time in putting together a system of payoffs and other illegal activi-ties to make himself rich.

Becker formed an association with Bald Jack Rose, a leading Jewish gambler and impresario with political connections. It was Jack's job to collect for what became known throughout the underworld as the "Becker pocketbook." Brothel madams, gambling operators and after-hours saloonkeepers all con-tributed to the Becker pocketbook, or they were raided and shut down. Bald Jack Rose would later claim that in ten months he and his lieutenants had collected $640,000 for Becker. This translates to about $10 million today.

Among the gamblers of the Lower East Side were a few noted for their talkativeness as well as their violence. Having made deals with Becker, these "holler guys" or "motor mouths" as they were called, felt free to complain whenever they didn't receive the special treatment they felt entitled to. One such holler guy was Herman (Beansy) Rosenthal who was a small-time, Jewish bookmaker and gambling club operator often in trouble with the law or with other gamblers. After a number of failed attempts to open a profitable gambling establishment, he allegedly became partners with Becker in a new gambling club on West 54th Street near Broadway.

By this time Becker was a lieutenant and making money hand over fist. In his partnership with Rosenthal he initially made money as well and everything was good. But he was enraged when Rosenthal would not kick in with a $500 "donation" to the defense fund of Becker's press agent, who had been charged with killing a man during a dice game. Becker's squad raided Rosenthal's club and Rosenthal threatened to go to the district attorney and reveal all the wrongdoings that Becker was part of in the city. This "stupid move" as his friends called it, cost him his life. He was shot four times at close range outside of the Metropole Hotel on West 43rd Street in Manhattan.

A four-man hit team was arrested for committing the murder. They confessed to being paid by underworld boss Big Jack Zelig, a well-known Jewish criminal figure from the lower East Side. Zelig was arrested and fingered Bald Jack Rose and Lt. Charles Becker as having given the contract for the murder of Rosenthal. Months later, just before Becker's trial for murder, Zelig was shot and killed on 13th Street in Manhattan. Even without Zelig as a witness, the case against Becker was very strong and he was convicted of murder and sentenced to death.

In many ways Becker was a victim of his time as much as anything else. Whether or not he was actually guilty remains an open question. Yet his sinister ties with The Tenderloin underworld cannot be denied. Becker had at least two things against him: a blindly ambitious District Attorney who astutely saw a death sentence for Becker as a free pass to the Governor's Mansion, and a hostile press dedicated to expose the police department in any way possible.

There was certainly no dearth of things in need of cleansing in New York City during Becker's time. The politics and the police were not unsullied. The Tenderloin, the area now known as Times Square, which is centered at 42nd Street and Broadway, had hundreds of gambling casinos and was under siege by a virtual army of prostitutes. Some estimates put the number of streetwalkers as high as 30,000. Since prostitution and gambling were illegal, it was common practice for pimps and casino owners to seek protection from prosecution by paying off the Police Department.

The police colluded openly with politicians at City Hall. The casino owners who refused to pay were promptly raided and put out of business. Public corruption was nothing new to New York. It had been going on for decades, interrupted now and then when an outraged citizenry called for reform. Under Tammany Hall, though, corruption reached its apex. From the lowly cop on the street to the highest echelons of City Hall itself, money talked. No city permit could be secured, no building could start and no business could open unless the right person received his payoff. Graft permeated every level of the bureaucratic structure.

In the days prior to July 30, 1915, Becker's supporters grew frantic. There were several organizations attempting to persuade the Governor to commute the sentence, and Becker's defense attorney, Cockran, tried a last-ditch effort to bring the case before the State Supreme Court. It too failed.

In a final declaration of innocence, Becker wrote a letter to the Governor. In it he denied murdering Herman Rosenthal, having procured his murder, or having any knowledge of the crime whatsoever. His personal appeal was unsuccessful, and

on July 30, 1915, Charles Becker became the first and only
New York City police officer to be executed.

In addition to working as a United States Attorney, Mauskopf is
active in various professional organizations, and has lectured on
criminal justice topics at law schools, colleges, and to many law
enforcement and community groups.

The daughter of two holocaust survivors, she is also dedicated to
maintaining the legacy of holocaust remembrance and has been active
in support of survivors and their heritage.

Steve Pomerantz

Steve Pomerantz was clearly one of the highest-ranking Jewish people
ever to serve in the Federal Bureau of Investigation. There was another
person, Alex Rosen, who was also an Assistant Director and presumably Jewish as well. In addition, since Pomerantz's retirement, there
has been an Executive Assistant Director (a rank that did not exist
during Pomerantz's time) named John Solomon, who was presumably Jewish.

Steve Pomerantz began his career in the FBI as a field investigative special agent. He eventually retired after 27 years as the Assistant
Director for counterterrorism in the bureau.

Pomerantz grew up in a Jewish neighborhood in the Bronx. His
family was not particularly religious, and he describes them as "cul-
turally" Jewish. But he did have a Bar Mitzvah in 1955. He attended
college at NYU, and knew all along that he wanted to do something
with his life that was exciting and served his country. His dream was
to be a pilot so he joined the Air Force but wound up in the military
police as part of the officer corps.

While in the Air Force he got his first taste of Muslim anti-Semitism when he was denied entry into West Pakistan because his passport
listed his religion as Jewish. It was suggested to him that he obtain
a new passport and have Christian listed as his religion but he told

them to "get lost." He remained in the Air Force for five years until 1968. "I got out of the Air Force on a Friday and entered the FBI that following Monday," he says (S. Pomerantz, personal communication, June 18, 2004).

One of his first assignments was to Mobile Alabama to participate in the investigation of the Ku Klux Klan (KKK), which he did with glee. He could tell that the roots of the KKK ran deep in the south, in fact, they are traceable back to the war between the states.

At the end of the American Civil War certain members of Congress attempted to destroy the white power structure of the Rebel states. The Freeman's Bureau was established by Congress on 3rd March, 1865, and was designed to protect the interests of former slaves. This included helping them to find new employment and to improve their educational and health facilities. In 1866, the bureau spent $17,000,000 establishing 4,000 schools, 100 hospitals and providing homes and food for former slaves.

Attempts by Congress to extend the powers of the Freemen's Bureau was vetoed by President Andrew Johnson in February, 1866. In April 1866, Johnson also vetoed the Civil Rights Bill that was designed to protect freed slaves from Southern Black Codes (laws that placed severe restrictions on freed slaves such as prohibiting their right to vote, forbidding them to sit on juries, limiting their right to testify against white men, carrying weapons in public places and working in certain occupations).

In 1867, Congress passed the first Reconstruction Act. The South was now divided into five military districts, each under a major general. New elections were to be held in each state with freed male slaves being allowed to vote. The act also included an amendment that offered readmission to the Southern states after they had ratified the Fourteenth Amendment and guaranteed adult male suffrage. Johnson immediately vetoed the bill but Congress re-passed the bill the same day.

The first branch of the Ku Klux Klan was established in Pulaski, Tennessee, in May, 1866. A year later a general organization of local Klans was established in Nashville in April, 1867. Most of the leaders were former members of the Confederate Army, and the first Grand Wizard was Nathan Forrest, an outstanding general during the American Civil War. During the next two years, Klansmen wearing masks, white cardboard hats and draped in white sheets, tortured and killed black Americans and sympathetic whites. Immigrants, who they blamed for the election of Radical Republicans, were also targets of their hatred. Between 1868 and 1870 the Ku Klux Klan played an important role in restoring white rule in North Carolina, Tennessee and Georgia.

At first the main objective of the KKK, as well as other white supremacy organizations (such as the White Brotherhood, the Men of Justice, the Constitutional Union Guards and the Knights of the White Camelia), was to stop black people from voting and to continue undermining the power of all African-Americans. Successful African-American businessmen were attacked, and any attempt to form black protection groups such as trade unions were quickly dealt with.

In the 1950s the emergence of the Civil Rights Movement resulted in a revival in Ku Klux Klan organizations. The most of important of these was the White Knights of the Ku Klux Klan led by Robert Shelton. In the Deep South considerable pressure was put on blacks by klansmen not to vote. An example of this was the state of Mississippi. By 1960, 42%

of the population were black but only 2% were registered to vote. Lynching was still employed as a method of terrorizing the local black population.

On Sunday, September 15, 1963, a white man was seen getting out of a white and turquoise Chevrolet car and placing a box under the steps of the Sixteenth Street Baptist Church. Soon afterwards, at 10.22 a.m., a bomb exploded killing Denise McNair (11), Addie Mae Collins (14), Carole Robertson (14) and Cynthia Wesley (14). The four girls had been attending Sunday school classes at the church. Twenty-three other people were also hurt by the blast.

A witness identified Robert Chambliss, a member of the Ku Klux Klan, as the man who placed the bomb under the steps of the Sixteenth Street Baptist Church. He was arrested and charged with murder and possessing a box of 122 sticks of dynamite without a permit. On October 8, 1963 Chambliss was found not guilty of murder and received a hundred-dollar fine and a six-month jail sentence for having the dynamite.

In 1964, the NAACP, the Congress of Racial Equality (CORE), and the Student Nonviolent Coordinating Committee (SNCC), organized its Freedom Summer campaign. Its main objective was to try and end the political disenfranchisement of African Americans. Volunteers from the three organizations decided to concentrate its efforts in Mississippi. The three organizations established 30 Freedom Schools in various towns throughout the state, and volunteers taught in the schools with curriculums that included black history and the philosophy of the civil rights movement. During the summer of 1964 over 3,000 students attended these schools and the experiment provided a model for future educational programs such as Head Start.

Unfortunately, Freedom Schools were often targets of white mobs. So also were the homes of local African Americans involved in the campaign. That summer 30 black homes and 37 black churches were firebombed. Over 80 volunteers were beaten by white mobs or racist police officers, and three men, James Chaney, Andrew Goodman and Michael Schwerner, were murdered by the Ku Klux Klan on June 21, 1964. These deaths created nation-wide publicity for the campaign.

One of the FBI's favorite tactics, according to Pomerantz, was to infiltrate the Klan or use informants. "We would go to the cross burnings at night when a new member was initiated" and then the next day agents would go to the new member's place of work and say loudly so everyone could hear "How was the Klan initiation last night?" This kind of public embarrassment was proof that the bureau "was there" and had a significant effect on decreasing Klan membership (S. Pomerantz, personal communication, June 18, 2004).

On May 17, 2000, the FBI announced that the Sixteenth Street Baptist Church Bombing had been carried out by the Ku Klux Klan splinter group, the Cahaba Boys. It was claimed that four men, Robert Chambliss, Herman Cash, Thomas Blanton and Bobby Cherry had been responsible for the crime. Cash was dead but Blanton and Cherry were arrested. In May 2002 the 71 year old Bobby Cherry was convicted of the murder of Denise McNair, Addie Mae Collins, Carole Robertson and Cynthia Wesley and was sentenced to life in prison.

Earlier in his career, Pomerantz served as the Assistant Director in charge of the Administrative Services Division of the FBI, where he was responsible for all personnel and financial matters in the bureau. He also served as Assistant Director in charge of the Criminal Justice Information Services Division, which is the single largest organizational entity in the FBI. This division provides criminal justice information services to virtually every domestic law enforcement and criminal justice agency in the United States as well as many abroad.

In 1982, following an explosion of terrorist incidents worldwide, FBI director William H. Webster made counterterrorism a national priority while maintaining the bureau's commitment to its other central missions including foreign counterintelligence, organized crime, and white-collar crime. In fact, the FBI solved so many espionage cases during the mid-1980s that the press dubbed 1985 "the year of the spy." One of the most serious cases of espionage damage uncovered by the FBI during this time was committed by the "John Walker spy ring."

John Anthony Walker Junior, born July 28, 1937, was a Chief Warrant Officer and communications specialist for the U.S. Navy, who sold his services as a spy to the Soviet Union from 1968 to 1985, at the height of the Cold War. In this time he helped the Soviets decipher over one million classified encrypted naval messages, and most observers agree that he was one of the most effective and destructive Soviet spies in US history.

Walker had begun spying for the Soviets in early February 1968, when he was facing serious financial problems because a South Carolina bar/restaurant he was operating on the side was deeply in debt and failing fast. So he simply walked into the Soviet Embassy in Washington, DC and sold a classified document (a radio cipher card) for a few thousand dollars. This was only the beginning of his 17 years of betrayal.

Walker would later try to justify his initial betrayal on the grounds that the classified Navy communications data he sold to the Soviets had already been completely compromised during the recent USS Pueblo incident (where a US Navy communications surveillance ship had been captured on the high seas by North Korea, its crew being held prisoner for nearly a year.)

Whenever Walker was transferred away from assignments where his handlers required information, he would recruit friends and members of his own family (his wife, his older brother Arthur and his son, Michael) to join in his spying activity. His friend and fellow spy was a Navy senior chief radioman named Jerry Whitworth, who had access to highly-classified satellite communications data. The resulting Walker Spy Ring continued to provide important intelligence to the Soviets even after John Walker had retired from the Navy in 1976.

Walker's activities went completely unsuspected by US authorities, despite his living quite extravagantly with his only source of visible income being his Navy pension.

Living in Norfolk, Virginia after his retirement, Walker became a licensed private investigator and a private airplane pilot, both of which he conveniently used to explain his lavish lifestyle and frequent journeys all over North America and to Western Europe (mainly to meet his Soviet handler for instructions and to receive payment.) As additional cover, he also joined right-wing political organizations such as the John Birch Society and the Ku Klux Klan. It is estimated that Walker earned more than 1 million dollars from nearly two straight decades of spying.

In May 1985, Walker and his accomplices were arrested on suspicion of espionage by the FBI. Six months before, Walker's ex-wife, weary of years of neglect by her ex-husband, and with Walker's refusal to pay her alimony being the last straw, finally turned the spy in. He was tried for and convicted of espionage and received multiple life prison terms. His son, Michael Walker, who had a relatively minor role in the ring and turned state's evidence in exchange for a reduced sentence, was released from prison on parole in February 2000.

Some researchers believe Walker's nearly two decades of spying contributed strongly to the unprecedented accession of then-KGB director Yuri Andropov (whose agents had overseen Walker's activities) to the Soviet premiership after the November 1982 death of Leonid Brezhnev, as well as helping precipitate the Soviets' controversial September 1, 1983 shootdown of Korean Air Flight 007 near the Kamchatka Peninsula.

After his arrest and conviction, Walker had no remorse. He enjoyed the publicity. He related that he had lived every fantasy that he ever had, and had done everything he wanted to do. He rationalized involving his brother, son and friend in espionage, and trying to recruit his daughter. In his mind, he was helping them be successful in life (i.e., earn lots of money), and he later criticized them for using him. He felt his only real mistake in life was allowing himself to be surrounded by weaker people who eventually brought him down. In the end, he concluded that he himself was the only real victim.

Although he took pride in being described as the most damaging spy in the history of the United States, Walker claimed to be a patriotic American. He viewed the Cold War as an unimportant game. He "knew" there would be no hot war with the Soviet Union, and he "knew" the Soviets would not risk passing his information to the North Vietnamese during the Vietnam war, so he rationalized his actions by stating that the compromise of military information was really doing little damage.

During the 1980s, in addition to espionage, narcotics and the illegal drug trade was a significant drain on the FBI's resources. To ease these demands, in 1982 the Attorney General gave the FBI concurrent jurisdiction with the Drug Enforcement Administration (DEA) over narcotics violations in the United States. The expanded Department of Justice attention to drug crimes resulted in the confiscation of millions of dollars in controlled substances, the arrests of major narcotics figures, and the dismantling of important drug rings.

One of the most publicized cases, dubbed "the Pizza Connection" case, involved the heroin trade in the United States and Italy. It resulted in 18 convictions, including a former leader of the Sicilian Mafia. Then Assistant U.S. Attorney Louis J. Freeh, who was to be appointed FBI Director in 1993, was key to the successful prosecution of this case.

On May 26, 1987, Judge Webster left the FBI to become Director of the Central Intelligence Agency. Executive Assistant Director John E. Otto became Acting Director and served in that position until November 2, 1987. During his tenure, Acting Director Otto designated drug investigations as the FBI's fifth national priority.

On November 2, 1987, former federal Judge William Steele Sessions was sworn in as FBI Director. Prior to his appointment as FBI

Director, Sessions served as the Chief Judge of the U.S. District Court for the Western District of Texas. He had previously served as a District Judge and as U.S. Attorney for that district.

Under Director Sessions, the FBI reassessed its strategies in defending national security, now no longer defined as the containment of communism and the prevention of nuclear war. Pomerantz was appointed as Chief of Counterterrorism. In that capacity, he was responsible for supervision of all FBI counterterrorism investigations both domestically and around the world. He was also extensively involved in law enforcement and intelligence liaison work as part of the world-wide effort to combat terrorism.

This new threat to national (and international) security became abundantly clear to the FBI on December 21, 1988 when Pan Am Flight 103 was blown up as it flew over Lockerbie, Scotland, killing 270 people from 21 countries.

Known as the Lockerbie bombing, it was regarded as an assault on a symbol of the United States, and with 189 of the victims being Americans, it stood as the deadliest attack on American civilians until September 11, 2001.

After a three year joint investigation by the Scottish Dumfries and Galloway Constabulary and the Federal Bureau of Investigation, during which 15,000 witness statements were taken, indictments for murder were issued on November 13, 1991, against Abdelbaset Ali Mohmed Al Megrahi, a Libyan intelligence officer and the head of security for Libyan Arab Airlines (LAA), and Al Amin Khalifa Fhimah, the LAA station manager in Luqa Airport, Malta.

On January 31, 2001, Megrahi was convicted of murder by a panel of three Scottish judges, and sentenced to 27 years in prison. Fhimah was acquitted. Megrahi's appeal against his conviction was refused on March 14, 2002, and a further appeal to the European Court of Human Rights was declared inadmissible in July 2003. He is serving his sentence in Greenock prison near Glasgow, where he continues to protest his innocence.

Between 1988 and 1998, Pomerantz and the FBI had to confront yet a new kind of terrorism – Islamic extremists.

At 12:18 PM on February 26, 1993, a huge bomb went off beneath the two towers of the World Trade Center. This was not a suicide attack. The terrorists parked a truck bomb with a timing device on Level B-2 of the under- ground parking garage, then departed. The ensuing explosion opened a hole up seven stories high.

Six people died and more than a thousand were injured in the World Trade Center blast. President Bill Clinton ordered his National Security Council to coordinate a response, and the New York Field office of the FBI took control of the local investigation. The fact the FBI field office did so well to quickly solve this case may have lent a false sense of security over the potential for such a thing happening again. Within days, the FBI identified a rental truck remnant. Mohammed Salameh was arrested when he returned to Ryder to get back his $400 deposit. In short order, the FBI had several conspirators in custody. These led the Bureau to a mosque in Brooklyn where Omar Abdel Rahman called "The Blind Sheikh" had been preaching hatred and planning to bomb other New York landmarks.

The investigation and subsequent convictions of most of those involved in the World Trade Center bombing obscured the need to examine the character and extent of the new threat facing the United States, and the ability of the government to collect and share intelligence to limit that threat. The fundamental orientation of law enforcement towards "reaction" as opposed to "pro-action" or preemption, needed to be changed.

"I've done everything there is to do in the FBI," says Pomerantz. But one of the best things he did was in 1982 when he met his wife Karen. Although not Jewish when they met, she had always been interested in Judaism and later officially converted. "After converting she became more of a religious Jew than I ever was" (S. Pomerantz, personal communication. June 18, 2004).

Since retiring from the FBI in 1995, Pomerantz has continued to work in the field of security and counter-terrorism. He is Vice President of the Institute for the Study of Terrorism and Political Violence, a non-profit international organization, and a consultant specializing in security and criminal justice related matters.

Pomerantz also serves as a Senior Professional with The Jewish Institute for National Security Affairs (JINSA), which is an independent, non-partisan, educational organization established in 1976 to fulfill various mandates: To educate the American public about the threats and dangers facing this country and its global allies; to explain why a mobile, technologically superior military is vital to America's security; to provide leadership on issues affecting American national security and foreign policy; to explain to Americans and others the importance of U.S. security cooperation with like-minded democratic partners around the world; and to explain the key role Israel plays in the Mediterranean and Middle East as an outpost of liberty, a linchpin of stability, and a friend and ally of the United States.

JINSA sponsors trips to Israel for active duty and eligible retired general and flag officers, where they participate in in-depth discussions with senior Israeli military and political leaders. It also sponsors a work/study program in Israel for American military cadets and midshipmen. In these symposia, future leaders of America's defense establishment participate in a three-week program that includes visits to major historical, religious and strategic areas. They also attend lectures and meet with Israeli military, political, and academic figures and work on a kibbutz.

JINSA also hosts numerous conferences, seminars and informal discussions every year. Subjects have run from proliferation of weapons of mass destruction and ballistic missile defense to terrorism and the impact of energy resources on security planning.

A Law Enforcement Exchange Program (LEEP) was established in 2002, and is designed to cement cooperation between American and Israeli law enforcement personnel and to give the American law enforcement community access to the hard "lessons learned" by the Israelis in the interdiction of and response to all forms of terrorism.

JINSA publishes *The Journal of International Security Affairs*, which contains topical articles by security and criminal justice professionals. A sample of articles in a recent edition of the Journal include "Jihad from Europe," "The Next Threat from Central Asia," "The Dynamics of Islamist Terror in South Asia," "The Legal Challenge to the War on Terror," and "Al-Qaeda Versus Democracy."

Pomerantz is interviewed often on matters of national security and counterterrorism. In one recent interview he was asked his opinion of the organization called Council on American Islamic Relations (CAIR) since mayor Bloomberg of New York City appointed a sympathetic member of CAIR, Omar Mohammedi, to New York City's Civil Rights Commission. According to Pomerantz, "CAIR originated from the Hamas front group, Islamic Association for Palestine (IAP), and has evolved into a propaganda arm for Hamas and other militant fundamentalists."

By appointing someone who is aligned with terrorists, Pomerantz pointed out, the Mayor is offering representation to a group that should be prosecuted vigorously. Such an appointment raises serious questions about the Mayor's motivations, and about what is going on at the City's Human Rights Commission.

Karen Tandy

Following nomination by President George W. Bush, Ms. Karen Tandy was sworn in September 16, 2003 as the Administrator of the Drug Enforcement Administration (DEA). She had been confirmed by unanimous consent in the U.S. Senate.

President Bush's nomination of Karen Tandy was applauded by many professionals in the criminal justice arena, including Karen Freeman Wilson, CEO of the National Association of Drug Court Professionals (NADCP). "It is critical to have someone at the helm of the DEA who recognizes the importance of, and who has the ability to, balance both treatment and enforcement. I believe that Karen Tandy has the integrity and commitment to accomplish this feat and to continue fostering the growth of the DEA. It is the full intent of NADCP to work cooperatively with her to achieve the mutual goal of reducing substance abuse and its concomitant crime," said Ms. Wilson (Wilson, 2003).

The NADCP is the principal organization of professionals involved in the development and implementation of treatment-oriented drug courts. Organized in 1994, NADCP represents more than 3,000 judges, prosecutors, defense attorneys, treatment providers and rehabilitation experts, law enforcement and corrections personnel, educators, researchers and community leaders. NADCP seeks to reduce substance abuse, crime and recidivism by promoting and advocating for the establishment and funding of drug courts and providing for collection and dissemination of information, technical assistance, and mutual support to association members.

Tandy made history when she became the first woman chosen to head the DEA. "Even today I sometimes have to pinch myself to make sure it's real when I think about how President Bush gave me a chance," she said in an interview with her alma mater Texas Tech University. "It was a surprise nomination any way you look at it," she explains. ". . . I didn't have any political connections in Washington, not to mention the fact that I come from a simple family in Texas. My mom was a secretary and my father was a regular employee at the telephone company. I am the first one in my entire family to finish college, and I graduated from schools in Texas and not from an Ivy League university." She finds it even more surprising that she is a "woman and the DEA is a male organization by nature, with a budget of $2 billion, 10,000 employees (half of which are armed agents), and 70 agencies in 150 countries" (Tandy, 2004).

Tandy knew that there were those who doubted the president's choice to nominate her. "I expected that the choice of a woman would get attention, but I was surprised that it was accepted almost naturally. It was clear that the employees of DEA were interested in strong leadership," says Tandy. Her selection of another woman to be her deputy also received a great deal of attention. But everybody in DEA saw that her skills were the best for the job. Nevertheless, some of the men in DEA seem to feel that one woman at the head of the organization is truly historical but two women are too much. Despite these concerns, says Tandy, "President Bush didn't even blink when I informed him of my choice for deputy" (K. Tandy, personal communication, April 10, 2004).

Prior to assuming her duties as DEA Administrator, Tandy was Associate Deputy Attorney General and Director of the Organized Crime Drug Task Forces (OCDETF). In this role, she was responsible for oversight of the Drug Enforcement Administration and the National Drug Intelligence Center. She was also responsible for developing national drug enforcement policy and strategies.

The roughly $500 million OCDETF program, which Tandy managed from January 2001 through July 2003, spanned three U.S. Departments and included more than 2,200 federal agents, 500 federal prosecutors, and various state and local law enforcement task forces around the country. Under Tandy's leadership, OCDETF refocused its efforts towards dismantling major drug trafficking and money laundering organizations. During her tenure at OCDETF, financial investigations increased from 16 percent to 59 percent; deposits to the Department of Justice Assets Forfeiture Fund increased by 33 percent; criminal charges against leadership-level defendants increased by 10 percent; and multi-jurisdiction cases increased from nine percent to 84 percent of the OCDETF investigations. In addition, the OCDETF program received a funding enhancement for the first time in 10 years.

Between 1990 and 1999, Tandy served in a variety of positions in the Criminal Division of the Department of Justice. She supervised the Department's drug and forfeiture litigation, and represented the Department of Justice before Congress in the successful effort to reform civil forfeiture law. As the first Chief of the Litigation Unit in the Asset Forfeiture Office, Ms. Tandy developed the Justice Department's expedited settlement policy to reduce unnecessary litigation for mortgage holders of forfeitable property. She also authored a criminal forfeiture practice handbook relied on by federal prosecutors throughout the country. As Deputy Chief of the Narcotics and Dangerous Drug Section, she supervised the Department's narcotic prosecutions nationwide. As the first Deputy Chief at the Special Operations Division, she had responsibility for implementing the nationwide coordination of drug wiretap investigations among federal prosecutors.

From 1979 to 1990, Ms. Tandy was an Assistant United States Attorney in the Eastern District of Virginia and in the Western District of Washington, handling the prosecution of violent crime and complex drug, money laundering, and forfeiture cases. During her almost 10 years in the Eastern District of Virginia, Ms. Tandy was named Senior Litigation Counsel and served as Chief of the Narcotics Section and Lead OCDETF Attorney. One of her OCDETF prosecutions led to the landmark U.S. Supreme Court Decision that attorney' fees are subject to forfeiture notwithstanding the Sixth Amendment Right to Counsel.

During 1988 to 1990, Tandy was Chief of the Asset Forfeiture Unit in the United States Attorney's Office in the Western District of Washington. She has lectured extensively on forfeiture law and practice, conducted international training, and developed a forfeiture teaching model for the American Bar Association. Prior to joining the Justice Department, she clerked for the Chief Judge of the Northern District of Texas.

Tandy, a native of Fort Worth Texas, grew up in a neighborhood with absolutely no Jews. With the goal of becoming a teacher, she attended Texas Tech University. However, the financial promise of teaching was not very bright so she decided to apply to Texas Tech Law School. She graduated in 1977 as one of the very few women in her class.

"The news [of Tandy's appointment to head DEA] came as no surprise," said Texas Tech Law School Dean Walter Huffman, who graduated from the law School with Tandy in 1977. "In our third year she was president of the SBA," Huffman said of Tandy. "It was indicative of the fact that even then she had the leadership qualities that would make her stand out . . . it's a real feather in the cap of the law school" (Huffman, 2003).

As DEA Administrator, Tandy has a particular interest in America's youth. She is gratified that teens are smoking less, but concerned that they are taking more pills. The lure of the family medicine cabinet may have been too much to resist for the nearly one in 10 high school seniors who try out prescription painkillers every year. A study of nearly 50,000 teens across the country found that 21.4 percent of eighth graders had used some illicit drug in their lives. For 10th graders it was 38.2 percent, and 12th graders it was 50.4 percent.

The use of the painkiller OxyContin grew from 4 percent to 5.5 percent of high school seniors from 2002 to 2005, and the use of Vicodin has been rising steadily and clocked in at 9.5 percent in 2005. Only marijuana topped prescription drugs in teen use, and that has been declining over time. For 2005, 44.8 percent of 12th graders said they had used marijuana at some time in their lives. The total was 34.1 percent for 10th graders, and 16.5 percent among eighth graders.

Tandy has warned of the increased availability of drugs through the Internet, which is certainly contributing to the abuse of drugs like OxyContin and Vicodin by teens and adults alike. In conjunction with the FDA, Tandy has implemented additional investigative efforts and enforcement actions against the illegal sale, use, or diversion of controlled substances, including those occurring over the Internet. Many of these "e-pharmacies" are foreign-based and expose the purchaser to potentially counterfeit, contaminated, or adulterated products.

Tandy sees criminals who divert legal drugs into the illegal market as no different from a cocaine or heroin dealer peddling poisons on the street corner. The DEA is aggressively working to put an end to this illicit practice whether it occurs in doctors' offices or cyberspace, and ensure the integrity of our medical system. This new strategy incorporates education of medical professionals and consumers, outreach to businesses involved in Internet commerce, pharmaceutical manufacturers, and pharmacies, as well as increased investigation and enforcement activities.

The new programs include: careful consideration of labeling and commercial promotion of opiate drug products; ensuring wider dissemination of education and training on appropriate pain management and treatment procedures for physicians authorized to prescribe controlled substances; increasing the number of state Prescription

Monitoring Programs, which detect suspicious prescriptions and individuals redeeming prescriptions from multiple physicians ("doctor shopping") to identify abusers; and using web crawler/data mining technology to identify, investigate and prosecute "pill mills"—Internet pharmacies that provide controlled substances illegally.

Because agencies, organizations, and individuals at the state and local level are uniquely positioned to quickly identify and respond to prescription drug diversion and abuse trends, the strategy seeks to create and extend collaborative efforts outside of the Federal government.

"Drug abuse, in all its forms, is a societal issue that demands societal solutions," Surgeon General Richard H. Carmona has said in a Fox News interview. "By engaging health professionals, families, and support groups we can provide assistance to people of all ages and from all walks of life who may be at risk, and help those who have already fallen victim to an addiction recover" (Carmona, 2005).

As an example of these kinds of Internet-based activities, was the advertisement posted on July 16, 2003 by a Dr. Brij Bhushan Bansal introducing himself as a wholesale distributor and supplier of generic and branded medicines manufactured by top pharmaceutical companies in India.

Bansal, who also advertised Sildenafil Citrate (generic Viagra), even gave his address—Brij & Co. B-50 Kamla Nagar, Agra—unlike several others who preferred the anonymity of e-mails on the web.

Less than two years later, after a joint operation by the DEA and India's Narcotics Control Bureau (NCB), Bansal was arrested along with 19 others including his son and daughter for running perhaps the biggest illicit Internet pharmacy. They allegedly shipped psychotropic drugs, amphetamines and anabolic steroids directly to buyers without a prescription as is required by the US and Indian laws.

The ring had delivered as many as 2.5 million doses of narcotics, amphetamines and steroids every month to tens of thousands of American customers and others abroad. The group also sold lifestyle drugs such as Viagra, but traded mostly in DEA-controlled substances. Tandy said it was especially disturbing that a relative handful of people could illegally divert such large quantities of potentially dangerous drugs. She revealed that the ring was based in Philadelphia and ran primarily by two Temple University students from India — one studying computers and the other probably medicine.

Regarding the personal side of Tandy's life, she met her husband Steve Pomerantz in 1984 when she worked for the Department of Justice Organized Crime Task Force. Steve served as Deputy Assistant Director of the FBI. She feels that it was somehow by a divine hand that they met. They were married on November 2, 1985 in Alexandria, Virginia.

Although her two daughters have been raised Jewish it was not until 1999 that Ms. Tandy officially converted to Judaism. She had been thinking about converting for quite some time but it was not until one of her daughters described herself in school as being "half Jewish" that she decided to finally do it. Her two daughters have attended Jewish Day Schools and have a solid and strong identity with being Jewish.

"I am a spiritual person," says Tandy, "and I believe that Judaism has been my destiny since childhood. Even my given name is Jewish. For my husband and me it was important to raise our daughters in a household of a single religion and clear identity. Slowly Judaism has entered our hearts and our home. The process that I went through took time, but I am happy and at peace with my decision. It also strengthened my sense of motherhood and family, and today I feel that Judaism is an inseparable part of who Karen Tandy is" (K. Tandy, personal communication, April 10, 2004).

One of the changes that Tandy has made at DEA is to insure that all official prayers and convocations are inclusive of all faiths, and she has taken "Jesus" out of all official services. Furthermore, if you want to eat in the DEA cafeteria, you can forget about ham or pork because these fares are no longer on the menu.

In 2004, Tandy made her first official visit to Israel as the head of the DEA, and her fifth visit in total. She sees Israel as an important alley of the United States in bringing to light the nexus between drugs and terror. Tandy sees much of the war on drugs as depending on cooperation between countries, such as the successful cooperation that we have today between the United States and Colombia, and between the United States and Israel. She is particularly aware that international terrorism is financed in part by the drug trade. This money has been used to finance the *intifada*, *Hamas*, and other fundamentalist and violent Islamic organizations."

Karen Tandy is a warm and soft-spoken Jewish woman who carries herself with almost majestic class. She is a self-proclaimed "Earth Mother" who cares intensely about people and causes. She is a strong leader and a tough prosecutor. She is also an ardent Zionist. At the height of the terror attacks in Israel, she and her husband agreed to allow one of their daughters to go there upon her request. "Had she wanted to travel anywhere else in the world under similar circumstances, we would not have agreed, but when it came to Israel, we clearly had to let her go because Israel is her place" (K. Tandy, personal communication, April 10, 2004).

Tandy sees herself as a mother above everything else. She and her husband divide up the chores on a daily basis, he makes dinner and she prepares breakfast. To manage this plus get to work, she gets up every morning at 4:30 A.M. Nevertheless, it's worth it for Tandy in order to keep some semblance of normalcy in her home and be involved on a daily basis with her children's lives. One of the only things she is prevented from doing, is attending parent-teacher conferences because of her security detail. "The constant presence of bodyguards is the highest price that my family pays," says Tandy.

Much of Ms. Tandy's marvelous spirit, commitment to law enforcement and to the Jewish people was captured in her address at the National Police Week Kaddish Service in Washington, D.C. in 2004. It is presented here in its entirety.

I want first to congratulate the D.C. Shomrim chapter on the occasion of your 50th anniversary. All of you, from chapters all over the country, honor the very heart of Shomrim: law enforcement officers of the Jewish faith joining together as guardians for the welfare of all. I have been part of law enforcement for more than a quarter century, and every day, I have the privilege of seeing the men and women in law enforcement secure our nation's safety and create a future of hope for our children. As law enforcement officers, we have dedicated ourselves as guardians of the foundations of freedom. Often it calls for sacrifice. Like you, there is not a day that passes that I don't think about the dangers agents and officers confront and the perilous evil that is ours to defeat.

Today we pay special tribute to those who sacrificed their life to safeguard our right to live in peace and safety. At last night's candlelight vigil, 362 names were added to this law enforcement memorial. Those men and women, and all the fallen officers we honor today, died in different circumstances and at different times, but they all died guarding our liberty and the rule of law. What an extraordinary nation we live in, that could have produced such brave and dedicated souls.

As our faith teaches us, their sacrifice was in pursuit of our most worthy goals: securing and protecting justice and equitable treatment for all people no matter their walk in life or economic circumstances.

I was interviewed recently and asked my view whether it is incongruous for Jews to serve in law enforcement. I was nonplussed by this question, a question so clearly rooted in stereotype ignoring history and reality. How can such a question even be posed when it was the Jewish people who were the very beginning of law enforcement as it has evolved today?

And, it is especially fitting that Jews, who historically and today have been victims of the most insidious and gruesome forms of *in*justice, are steadfastly committed in this hour to achieving justice and fair treatment for *all* people.

The Shomrim commitment to justice began long ago. Far longer ago, it was God who instilled in us the pursuit of equity and justice as he led the Jewish people from tyranny in Egypt. It was God, in his infinite wisdom in handing down his commandments and laws, created our police force, by commanding in Deuteronomy that mankind establish judges and officials "at all thy gates." And it was God who not once but twice declared "Justice, justice shall you pursue" as he pronounced that judges and police officials "shall govern the people with due justice. You shall not judge unfairly; you shall show no partiality; you shall not take bribes, for bribes blind the eyes of the discerning and upset the plea of the just. Justice, justice shall you pursue, that you may thrive and occupy the land the Lord your God is giving you."

It was the Jewish people who introduced the central concept that guides our President as he seeks justice: that our rule of law is divinely inspired. In protecting and following the rule of law, we are not just keeping a social order that was thrown together by accident.

Instead, we are ensuring that we live the moral lives God intended when he delivered the Ten Commandments to Moses.

This is an awesome burden for law enforcement officers. We confront powerful evil forces who often outnumber us and outgun us, who often possess far greater wealth than our police forces, who often gain added strength through corruption, and who are not constrained by morals, a sense of right and wrong, or the laws that we protect.

A couple of months ago, I stood in Florence, Italy, before Michelangelo's statue of David – one of the greatest Jews who ever lived – King David, who gave us the Book of Psalms and founded the holy city of Jerusalem.

As Michelangelo completed this masterpiece 500 years ago, he depicted a young David – tall, taut and determined – in the tense moment before his battle with Goliath.

As the Israelite troops nearest Goliath were fleeing in terror, David, the youngest child among eight brothers – and nothing more than a shepherd boy – stepped forward to confront a force far mightier than he. He stood virtually naked, armed only with a stick, a sling, and a few river rocks. He faced Goliath, nine feet tall, covered in 130 pounds of heavy armament, and bearing a sword, spear, and javelin.

As we all know from the Bible story, David slew Goliath with just his sling. Yet, on the statue of David, that sling is barely visible – draped unremarkably over his shoulder to remind us that he owed his victory not to brute force, which was the monopoly of his enemy, but to his intellect, his innocence, and his faith in God. As the inscription states under the statue – "David is the symbol of liberty and civic pride, a young hero who, through unshakable belief in God, defeated a more powerful foe."

We in law enforcement today are the Davids fighting Goliath. Today's Goliath, or would-be Goliath, comes in many guises: a drug cartel, a terrorist network, and gangs preying on our children and our neighborhoods. But each day that we stand the thin blue line that separates good from evil, we bring peace and security to all people, and honor to the sacrifice of our fallen partners.

In the circle of life, it is the memory of our fallen heroes that inspires us to stand the line. Our courageous warriors on this wall – and on every law enforcement Wall of Honor – are now safe in God's keeping, but they will always remain in our hearts as our inspiration, our moral compass, and surely, our Guardian Angels.

In keeping with the rich Jewish tradition of observing Yahrzeit, our prayers and remembrances at today's service mark the "law enforcement" anniversary of the death of our fallen comrades, echoing 4,000 years of tradition, for the Jewish people and for all freedom-loving people. May God bless and protect you all, and

God bless America (May 14, 2004).

Eli Rosenbaum

As Director of the Office of Special Investigations with the United States Department if Justice, Eli Rosenbaum is the longest-serving prosecutor and investigator of Nazi war criminals in world history.

As a child growing up on Long Island, Rosenbaum's father one day revealed that as an Army intelligence officer in World War II he had entered Dachau just a day after its liberation. When attempting to discuss what he saw at the concentration camp, his father "opened his mouth as if to speak but nothing came out and tears welled up in his eyes," said Rosenbaum. "My father's inability to talk about what he saw spoke volumes to me, as a youngster, about the magnitude of the horrors that had been perpetrated." To this day Rosenbaum keeps a copy of his father's orders sending him to Dachau on the wall of his office at the Justice Department (E. Rosenbaum, personal communication, January 15, 2006).

As a law student at Harvard, Rosenbaum read a book by Journalist Howard Blum about the search for Nazis in America. He remembers how angry he was to learn that people who had committed genocide had come to the United States, and that our government wasn't doing anything about it.

Rosenbaum realizes that the Holocaust is a catastrophe of such immense and horrific proportions that it is almost too difficult to be absorbed, much less comprehended. But it is the mandate of the Office of Special Investigations (OSI) to deal with the reality of the acts which accomplished the near-total destruction of European Jewry.

Following World War II, many countries were generous in accepting immigrants from war-torn Europe. These countries included the United States, Australia, Canada and England, which collectively took in hundreds of thousands of displaced persons. But Rosenbaum makes it clear that these countries also took in thousands of people who were implicated in the Holocaust and other Nazi crimes. In the United States during the 1950s and 1960s occasional prosecutions of war criminals were attempted which sought citizenship revocation or deportation. But most war criminals felt safe that they had gotten away unpunished for their horrible crimes against eight million European Jews.

Rosenbaum points to the work of one person whose courageous efforts helped insure that Nazi war criminals did not get away with their atrocities. This person was New York congresswoman Elizabeth Holtzman who facilitated congressional hearings in 1977 and 1978 resulting in the enactment of a law now known as the Holtzman Amendment. This law rendered individuals who took part in Nazi crimes against humanity under the Nuremberg charter excludable from the United States.

In 1979, a New York Times article was published addressing the large number of former Nazis living in this country. It motivated the government to take action.

In response to the New York Times article and the efforts of Ms. Holtzman, The Carter Administration created a special unit within the Justice Department now known as the Office of Special Investigations to investigate and bring these criminals to justice.

When he saw a notice in the paper announcing the opening of the OSI, Rosembaum called the then director Mark Richard and arranged to be the unit's very first summer law school intern. He already had an M.B.A. from the Wharton School and had planned on a career in corporate law or the business world, but after working at OSI for the summer, he knew that he wanted to go back.

In the third year of law school at Harvard, Rosenbaum wrote a paper on the prosecution of Nazi war criminals and the Holtzman Amendment. At about that time he also noticed that the statute of limitations on prosecuting Nazi war crimes was about to expire in Germany, so he led the school's Jewish Law Students Association in a campaign to obtain signatures of protest from law professors all over the country. He also convinced Halmut Schmidt, chancellor of West Germany, who was addressing Harvard's graduating class that year, to meet with him. Soon after, the German Parliament extended the statute of limitations indefinitely.

As a trial attorney at OSI, Rosenbaum has served as co-counsel on numerous major cases. In 1983 he played an instrumental role in the prosecution and first deportation of a Nazi criminal from the United States in more than 30 years. He also initiated and directed the Justice Department's investigation of Arthur L.H. Rudolph, the former Project Director of NASA's Saturn V rocket program who fled to West Germany in 1984 rather than contest war crimes charges in this country.

Rosenbaum admits that his job is not a pleasant one, in fact, it can be intensely painful. In 1982 he worked for two weeks in Israel interviewing survivors of Hitler's death camps. All day long he talked to these old people, who held within their memories and their souls the most horrific events imaginable that human beings could do to other human beings. He felt guilty doing this and asking the questions that he needed to ask. "I knew it would result in pain and tears," says Rosenbaum but it was something that had to be done in order to bring murderers to justice.

At times during these tortured interviews, victims would look at him and say with fear and hopelessness in their voice, "I have already told this to the German authorities." Rosenbaum reassured them with "I am not German, I am an American." He did not have to tell them that he was a Jew like them – it was understood (E. Rosenbaum, personal communication, January 15, 2006).

One thing that Rosenbaum has struggled with from the early days of the OSI has been whether it is an asset or a liability that he is himself Jewish. His "Jewishness" became an issue right from the beginning, even during his interview for the position of Director of OSI.

The interview was "four eyes only" (consisting of only two people) and one of the questions he was asked was, "How would you avoid zealotry in your work?" "I wanted to walk out of the room," says Rosenbaum. He questions why someone would expect him to be a "zealot?" Is it because he is Jewish? Would the same question be asked if he had not been a Jew? Would this question be asked of any other minority? But he controlled his anger and played the interviewer's game for one reason – or for nine million reasons – to be in the position to fight for justice for all those who never could.

This was not the last time he felt that being Jewish was an "issue" for others in the Justice Department. This would particularly come up during meetings with other federal prosecutors when discussing budgets. Rosenbaum looks around the room and can almost "feel" them thinking things like "Why are you spending so much on this Nazi hunter stuff?" But nobody has actually verbalized these thoughts (to his face). "If they had, I would tell them, sure they're investigating fraud, but I'm investigating millions of murders" (E. Rosenbaum, personal communication, January 15, 2006).

Today the Office of Special Investigations has the highest success rate of any component of the Justice Department's Criminal Division. Rosenbaum sees one of the main reasons for this as being the collapse of the former Soviet Union which opened up access to archives of evidence, which were never before available. Individuals whose names were previously unknown to OSI were identified and became suspects and eventually defendants. Researchers were allowed into archives, whose documents had previously been available only at the discretion of Soviet intermediaries. OSI was suddenly able to develop new cases and revive old ones that had reached dead ends.

Rosenbaum was working on one such case in 1983. Aleksandras Lileikis had been chief of the Lithuanian Security Police in Vilnius province during Nazi occupation. Since the 1950s he'd been living in Massachusetts. Only 5,000 of Vilnius' 60,000 Jews survived the war. Thousands were sent to Paneriai, a wooded hamlet outside of Vilnius, where they were stripped of their clothing, lined up in pits, and shot. Rosenbaum was eager to bring to justice a man believed to have ordered such atrocities and who, unlike many of the men OSI prosecutes, was not simply "a trigger puller." Rosenbaum confronted the 76-year-old in his home with a document that consigned 52 Jews to the killing squads in Paneriai. Although Lileikis' name was typed at the bottom of the page, the order was not signed, and Lileikis denied any knowledge of it. Rosenbaum remembers Lileikis' challenge: "Show me something I signed." Despite requests for documentation from the Soviet Union, nothing turned up, and the case that Rosenbaum wanted so badly to move forward lay dormant.

Ten years later, in 1993, OSI's senior investigative historian had gotten access to Lithuanian archives. As he sorted through records from the Lukiskes prison in Vilnius, he found what they'd been hoping for: order after order – sending Jews to prison, sending them to labor camps, handing them over to the killing squads – all signed by Aleksandras Lileikis. Rosenbaum, together with the civil division of the U.S. Attorney's Office, filed the case. They won on summary judgment and Lileikis was stripped of his citizenship and left the country rather than face deportation charges. He was put on trial in Lithuania for genocide, but the prosecution was never completed, ostensibly due to the poor state of Lileikis' health.

Within the United States, 59 participants in various Nazi crimes of persecution have been denaturalized as a result of OSI's efforts and 47 such individuals have been removed from the United States. OSI is also responsible for preventing war criminals from entering the

United States. Years of research have enabled the unit to identify more than 60,000 suspected European and Japanese participants in war crimes against humanity. The OSI has had the names of these individuals added to the government's border control watch list of aliens ineligible to enter the country. The program has resulted in over 200 Nazis (and one Japanese criminal) being turned back at U.S. airports.

Through the years Rosenbaum has been involved with numerous special projects at OSI, from a report on the United Nations' role in assisting Klaus Barbie, the Gestapo chief of Lyon, elude French authorities, to tracing the whereabouts of the horrible Josef Mengele. At one point in this investigation, pieces of Mengele's remains were stored in Rosenbaum's desk drawer, "an appropriate posthumous humiliation," he recalled (E. Rosenbaum, personal communication, January 15, 2006).

One of the projects for which Rosenbaum has received considerable praise involved an interagency investigation into gold and other assets that the Nazis had looted. He and OSI historians traced shipments of victim's gold to various European countries, including Switzerland. Most of these countries were able to be convinced to donate the value of at least part of the six tons of gold to a special fund for the victims of Nazi persecution.

Rosenbaum received considerable international attention for his success in bringing former Secretary General of the United Nations, and President of Austria, Kurt Waldheim to justice.

Kurt Waldheim was born December 21, 1918 at St. Andrä-Wördern in Austria. He joined the Austrian diplomatic service soon after the end of World War II in 1945, after finishing his studies in law at the University of Vienna. He served as First Secretary of the Legation in Paris, and then as the Ministry for Foreign Affairs in Vienna from 1951 to 1956. In 1956 he was made Ambassador to Canada, returning to the Ministry in 1960, after which he became the Permanent Representative of Austria to the United Nations in 1964. For two years beginning in 1968, he was the Federal Minister for Foreign Affairs in Austria serving for the Austrian People's Party, before going back as Permanent Representative to the U.N. in 1970. He was defeated in the Austrian presidential elections in 1971, but was then elected to succeed U Thant as United Nations Secretary-General the same year.

Waldheim was finally elected President of Austria in 1986 despite a series of articles appearing in the weekly newsmagazine *Profil* revealing that there had been several omissions about Waldheim's life between 1938 and 1945 in his recently-published autobiography. It was later revealed that Waldheim had lied about many aspects of his pre-war and war time activities including his service as an officer in the *SA-Reitercorps* as one of the *Sturmabteilung*. This unit, translated as the "Stormtroopers" functioned essentially as a paramilitary organization of the NSDAP – the German Nazi party. It played a key role in Adolf Hitler's rise to power in the 1930s. SA men were often known as brownshirts from the color of their uniform and to distinguish them from the SS who were known as blackshirts. The SA was also the first Nazi paramilitary group to develop pseudo-military titles for bestowal upon its members.

Waldheim had also incorrectly stated in his autobiography that he was wounded and had spent the last years of the war in Austria. But there was evidence that he was actually an ordinance officer in Saloniki, Greece during these final years. It was also well-documented that many crimes against civilians were committed during this occupation.

In his 1993 book *Betrayal*, Rosenbaum chronicled the hitherto untold story of the investigation of Kurt Waldheim and the subsequent infamous attempted cover-up. He recounted the full story of the "Waldheim Affair" as it would be called, which exposed the hidden Nazi past of the Secretary General and self-proclaimed "chief human rights officer of the planet Earth" (p. 12).

Rosenbaum revealed how it was possible for a deception of such magnitude to be perpetrated by a man who spent decades in the public eye. Rosenbaum literally spent years looking through thousands of European, American, and Israeli documents which revealed the truth about what Waldheim really did during his Nazi service in Hitler's Army.

As a federal prosecutor, Rosenbaum had been involved in some of the most difficult and sensitive investigations ever undertaken by the

United States Department of Justice. "Never, however, had I encountered anything like the Waldheim investigation," he states.

Part of Rosenbaum's investigation took him to Waldheim's birth place of Austria. About Austria he says in *Betrayal*:

> The average Austrian wishes the world to see his country as it was depicted in the earlier portions of *The Sound of Music*, with its sumptuous vistas and Catholic aristocrat hero. However, Austrian censors would undoubtedly prefer to snip out the last half hour of the film. The final portion – when German and Austrian Nazis dispel the myth of the Alpine paradise – depicts what so many Austrians do not wish the world to recall: the country's disproportionate role in the atrocities of World War II (p. 10).

Rosenbaum points out in the book that Hitler himself was Austrian, and that he recalled fondly in *Mein Kampf* that it was in Vienna where, for "a few pennies, I bought the first anti-Semitic pamphlet of my life." Indeed, Hitler said, "I came as a seventeen-year-old to Vienna . . . and left it as an absolute anti-Semite" (p. 11).

Adolf Eichmann, the architect of Hitler's genocidal "final solution" to the "Jewish question," was raised in Austria, and 80 percent of his staff was Austrian, as were about 75 percent of the concentration camp commandants. On July 24, 1944 Kurt Waldheim was a commander of the German High Command in Army Group E, Ic/AO. On that day more than 1,700 Jews living on the island of Rhodes were deported to the Nazi death camps in Auschwitz, Poland. "Upon arrival, most of them were immediately murdered in the gas chambers, their bodies promptly incinerated in the ovens and cremation pits. Neither infant nor invalid was spared" (Rosenbaum, 1993).

Today, in the town of Rhodes, the "Street of the Hebrew Martyrs" memorializes the spot on which the Jews of Rhodes were assembled by the Germans. "From there," Rosenbaum states, "they were marched to the waiting coal barges that took them away – forever – at [the] instruction of the High Command of Army Group E, Ic/AO" (p. 474).

Now, with many of its targets dead or dying (due to the "biologi-cal" solution), the Office of Special Investigations, under Rosenbaum, is being remade to take on additional tasks such as tracking down war criminals within the United States who have connections to other genocidal conflicts around the globe.

This new mission, included as part of the broad intelligence restruc-turing package was recently passed by Congress and signed by President Bush. Rosenbaum sees the expansion of the office as a reflec-tion of growing worldwide concern over the fate of suspected war criminals from the Balkans, Cambodia and elsewhere, many of whom have escaped prosecution by blending in with immigrant populations in the United States.

Human rights advocacy groups are hopeful the new mandate will allow the Justice Department to locate and prosecute more suspected war criminals who have found refuge in the United States.

The new legislation would allow OSI to seek to keep out or remove immigrants who "committed, ordered, incited, assisted or otherwise par-ticipated in conduct outside the United States" that would be considered genocide, acts of torture or extrajudicial killings. The legislation also calls for the authorization of enough money to ensure that OSI "fulfills its continuing obligations regarding Nazi war criminals" (Rosenbaum, 1999).

To date, Rosenbaum's office has won 81 cases against Nazi war criminals, has 60 cases under investigation, and 19 still in litigation.

Rosenbaum feels a strong sense of personal obligation to all sur-vivors of murder and genocide, but especially to the survivors of the Holocaust. "They are the true heroes of these cases," he said in an interview with *Lifestyles* magazine. "It is terribly painful for the sur-vivors to repeat their tragic stories in court. But time and again, they reopen their still-unhealed wounds in order to help us secure a measure of justice on behalf of the millions of silent accusers—the innocents who perished in the camps, forests, and ghettos." He adds, "Their former tormentors aren't fit to breathe the same air that they do, and they aren't fit to walk the same earth that the survivors and other decent Americans walk" (January 1999, p. 1).

Michael Chertoff

Michael Chertoff was sworn in as Secretary of Homeland Security on March 3, 2005. He was born November 28, 1953 an Israeli citizen (by virtue of his mother's Israeli citizenship) in Elizabeth, New Jersey, the son of Rabbi Gershon Baruch Chertoff and El Al's first flight attendant, Livia Eisen Chertoff. His grandfather was a Russian Jew.

Chertoff went to The Pingry School for high school. He later attended Harvard University, graduating in 1975. He graduated magna cum laude from Harvard Law School in 1978, going on to clerk for appellate judge Murray Gurfein for a year before clerking for United States Supreme Court justice William Brennan from 1979 to 1980. He worked in private practice with Latham & Watkins from 1980 to 1983 before being hired as a prosecutor by Rudolph Giuliani, then the U.S. attorney for Manhattan, working on mafia and political corruption-related cases.

In 1987, Chertoff joined the office of the U.S. Attorney for the state of New Jersey. He was appointed by President George H.W. Bush in 1990 as United States Attorney for the state in 1990. Chertoff was asked to stay in his position when the Clinton administration took office in 1993, he was the only U.S. attorney not replaced. As a federal prosecutor he oversaw high-profile prosecutions like that of Jersey City Mayor Gerald McCann and New York chief judge Sol Wachtler.

Mayor McCann served on the Jersey City council from 1977 to 1981 and as mayor of Jersey City twice - from 1981 to 1985 and from 1989 to 1992. He was removed from the mayor's office in 1992 after being convicted in federal court on federal charges of fraud and tax evasion. Chertoff was the lead prosecutor in the case.

In 1984, Sol Wachtler was pretty much on top of the world. After a successful career as a lawyer and Long Island politician, he was appointed as a trial judge by Governor Nelson Rockefeller in 1968. Four years later, he was elected to a judgeship on the highest court in the state, the New York Court of Appeals. In late 1984, Governor Cuomo appointed him to serve as Chief Judge of the court. His name was even mentioned as a possible Republican nominee for Vice-President or President. He was happily married with four children.

In 1984 he was named trustee of a trust established for Joy Silverman by her stepfather. Ms. Silverman was a socially prominent and attractive woman who was seventeen years younger than Wachtler. His fiduciary relationship with Ms. Silverman developed into an affair. In 1990, Wachtler experienced a major depression. Rather than seek professional help, he thought he could self-medicate by seeing different doctors and receiving prescriptions from all of them. None of the doctors were aware of the various medications he was taking.

As the depression worsened, Wachtler decided that he could deal better with his difficulties if he terminated his personal relationship with Ms. Silverman. After doing this, he had second thoughts about it. He realized that he missed the feeling of being needed by her and the gratification that he had received from helping her. When he attempted to resume a personal relationship with Ms. Silverman, she was not interested. When she informed Wachtler that she had begun a relationship with another man, he became intensely jealous.

His mental illness (later diagnosed as bipolar disorder), and the combination of medications that he was taking clouded his perception and judgment. He engaged in a bizarre series of behaviors that were designed to "win back" Ms. Silverman. He attempted to create situations that would cause her to conclude that she needed Wachtler's advice and support again. As each effort failed, Wachtler attempted something more bizarre than his previous efforts. Eventually, Ms. Silverman figured out who was orchestrating these events. Because they had begun to take on a threatening tone, she contacted law enforcement authorities.

One of Wachtler's tactics had been to pretend to be a man named David Purdy, who had harassed Ms. Silverman (in the hope that she would be prompted to call on Wachtler for help). When Wachtler (acting as Purdy) sent a letter to Joy Silverman's daughter demanding $20,000 to make him leave her alone, the FBI arrested Wachtler for extortion. Eventually, Wachtler pleaded guilty to mailing a threatening letter and was sentenced to a term of fifteen months in federal prison.

Psychology Today reported that in a letter to the *New York Times*, Chertoff, who was the prosecutor in the case, wrote that the FBI apprehended Wachtler on a New York expressway because there was a slight risk "that Mr. Wachtler could harm himself or others" if arrested at his home. "In fact," continued Chertoff, "the last place law enforcement officers want to arrest a potentially violent individual is at his home, where there may be weapons or where others may be placed in jeopardy" (August, 1997, p. 15).

As chief Republican counsel to the Senate Whitewater Committee during the administration of President Bill Clinton, Chertoff played a major role in the investigation of Clinton's Arkansas business dealings, and in the suicide of Vincent Foster, a Clinton aide and former law partner of Hillary Clinton.

Chertoff is the co-author, along with Viet Dinh, of the USA PATRIOT Act, signed into law October 26, 2001. As head of the Justice Department's criminal division, he advised the Central Intelligence Agency on the outer limits of legality in coercive interrogation sessions.

From 2001 to 2003, he headed the criminal division of the Department of Justice, leading the prosecution's case against terrorist suspect Zacarias Moussaoui. Chertoff was appointed to the Third Circuit Court of Appeals in Philadelphia by Bush on March 5, 2003, and was confirmed by the Senate 88-1 on June 9th.

In late 2004, after the controversial Bernard Kerik was forced to decline President Bush's offer to replace the outgoing Secretary of Homeland Security Tom Ridge, a lengthy search ensued to find a suitable replacement. Citing his experience with post-9/11 terror legislation, Bush nominated Chertoff to the post in January 2005. He was unanimously approved for the position of Secretary of the Department of Homeland Security (DHS) by the Senate on February 15, 2005.

Secretary Chertoff has developed innovative methods for dealing with the threats this country faces from terrorism. These have included a "six-point agenda" for the Department of Homeland Security designed to ensure that the Department's policies, operations, and structures are aligned in the best way to address the potential threats that this country faces.

In order to increase our overall preparedness, Chertoff has worked on creating better transportation security systems, strengthening border security and interior enforcement, enhancing information sharing with other security agencies, improving DHS human resource development and information technology, and realigning the DHS organization to maximize mission performance.

Chertoff sees our enemy as constantly changing and adapting, so the Department of Homeland Security (DHS)"must be nimble and decisive." He sees the priorities of the DHS as being risk-driven, and the goal of the DHS as being the maximization of our country's security but only to the extent that Americans' freedom, prosperity, mobility, and individual privacy are protected.

Sources

Carmona, R. (2005). Fox News. http://Foxnews.com (acquired April 25, 2005).

Epstein, R.K. Eli Rosenbaum: the hunter. *Lifestyles* magazine, vol. 27, No. 159, January, 1999.

Huffman, W. (2003). Texas Tech News. http://Texastech.edu (acquired February 3, 2005)

Pomerantz, S. (2004). *Personal Communication* (June 18, 2004).

Rosenbaum, E. (2006). *Personal Communication.* (January 15, 2006).

Tandy, K. (2004). Texas Tech News. http://Texastech.edu (acquired April 10, 2004).
Tandy, K. (2004). News Release. http://Whitehouse.gov (acquired November 27, 2005).

Tandy, K. *Speech at the National Police Week Kaddish Service*, May 14, 2004.

The Journal of Industrial Security Affairs, No. 9, Fall, 2005.

New York Times, March 8, 2000.

Psychology Today, August, 1997.

Rosenbaum, E.M. (1993). *Betrayal.* New York: St. Martins Press.

U.S. Department of Justice. (2004). U.S. Attorney's Office. http://Usdoj.gov (acquired March 5, 2005).

Wilson, K. (2003). Texas Tech News. http://Texastech.edu (acquired February 5, 2005).

http://businessofgovernment.org.

http://businessofgovernment.org/main/interviews/bios/tischler.

http://cbp.gov.

http://crimelibrary.com/gangsters_outlaws/cops_others/becker/1.html.

http://crimelibrary.com/terrorists_spies/spies/walker/1.html.

http://depts.ttu.edu.

http://ford.utexas.edu/library/exhibits/cabinet/levi.htm.

http://nadcp.org/publicrelations/karentandy.htm.

http://news.uchicago.edu/citations/00/000308./levi-nyt.html.

http://politicalgraveyard.com.

http://politicalgraveyard.com.

http://texastech.edu/news/currentNews/display_article.php?id=1417.

http://usfoj.gov/usao/nye/pr/2004nov22.htm.

http://whitehouse.gov/news/releases/2006/01/20060/03-3.html

Chapter 4

New York

Jacob Hays

Jacob Hays, the High Constable of New York in the early 19th century was known as a "police force all by himself" because of his habit of chasing criminals without assistance and suppressing riots whenever they sprung up. He was, perhaps, the best-known man of his time in the city, and was considered a "terror" to criminals. He would boast that there was not a rogue in the city whom he did not know.

Hays was born in May 1772 to a Jewish home in Bedford, New York. His father was a prominent member of the "Whig" party and a soldier in George Washington's army. As a youngster, Jacob's house was often used as a meeting place by General Washington and his officers and he was very comfortable around such notables.

Hays was first appointed New York Marshal by Mayor Varick in 1798. In 1802 he was appointed High Constable of New York by Mayor Livingston, and on March 21, 1803, he and another officer were appointed Captains of the Third Watch District in the fledgling police force.

Hays was considered a "master sleuth" of his day, and it is said that he believed he could distinguish the criminal physical build from that of the honest man. He was actually the first American detective of note, although in his time he was known as a "shadow" because the detective branch of the police department was not created in New York until 1857.

He is reported to have been an honest man of high moral character. But the office of constable did not continue to be held in such high regard in the future. In the 1830s and 1840s, the image of constable would become somewhat tarnished. Serving under magistrates or justices of the peace, constables made a habit of supplementing their official income (which was usually paid on a piecework basis) with "reward" money posted by victims of crimes. Indeed, notices were regularly posted at the police offices promising considerable sums of money for the recovery of property, This arrangement apparently made some constables rich.

In *Our Police Protectors: History of New York Police*, Augustine Costello cited an article in the Herald which denounced these practices. "A man may have his pocket robbed of a thousand dollars, and pay half that money to some of our Justices to recover the other half" (1875, p.1).

Hays' proclivity and proficiency for catching criminals was so great that his fame spread all over the civilized world. It was reported in *Our Police Protectors*, that he was as well known in London as he was in New York. It was also said at the time that he could "track a rogue by instinct."

Another fact about Hays is that he never carried a concealed weapon, his only protection being his Constable's staff and his own indomitable fearlessness of danger. He was reportedly "possessed of great physical strength" to the extent that few of the desperadoes of those days dared to cross his path. He often put down a street fight, "in which some of the worst factions were engaged" without having to use any force whatever (chapter 4, part 3, p. 2).

One of the secrets of his success was that he almost never used violence while dealing with a mob. He left no broken heads or bruised bodies which would inspire vengeance. "Fearlessness, firmness and forbearance were his predominant traits," and, as he never wantonly maltreated or injured any one, even in the face of great provocation. Brawlers and criminals rarely offered him much resistance. His great presence of mind and personal tact helped him in moments of peril and emergency. He generally minimized the seriousness of public outbreaks and declared them as being "misdeeds" or the "work of unruly boys." He was respectful of all people, even unruly ones, and would often be heard to say "Now, all good citizens, go home!" This advice seldom went unheeded (Chapter 4, part 3, p. 1).

On the Fourth of July, Hays always participated in the parade and was known to march in front of all the city officials shouldering a drawn sword, his hat decked with feathers, and his clothing decorated with the glittering insignia representative of his office.

Like most modern day police officers, High Constable Hays was always on the job even when officially off duty. One Fourth of July, while gathered for the ceremonial patriotic assemblage in front of the City hall, the City Fathers and the Mayor were giving Hays an award. He looked inpatient and was heard to say "Please hurry, there is a man out there in the crowd who answers a description I have in my pocket of a man for whose arrest there is offered a reward of five hundred dollars." The High Constable then disappeared in the crowd, and in the next moment returned, holding a tight grip on the suspect, whom he then marched off to jail.

Hays was also noted for his benevolence and philanthropy. While he never compromised with felons or law-breakers, he never used any illegitimate or unjust means to secure their conviction. He was firm yet moderate. He was intelligent, zealous about performing his duties, and incorruptible. He showed no malice and would not compromise his honor to serve his ambition.

No man hated crime or criminals more than Hays, and no man was more relentless in bringing criminals to justice. But if a criminal would repent and show a genuine desire to reform, he was always willing to stretch out a helping hand with mercy for his brother.

When High Constable Hays died at age seventy-eight, he was awarded full honors, and his funeral was attended by all the leading city dignitaries.

Otto Raphael

Otto Raphael was born in 1871 to Russian-Jewish immigrant parents. His father, who had been a butcher in Russia, settled on the lower East Side of Manhattan where he started out as a peddler until he could afford to open his own meat market around 1890. Raphael, who was one of several children, helped his father in the business.

In 1895 Otto and his father saved the lives of over twelve people who were caught in a burning tenement building near their house. Shortly thereafter, Otto met Theodore Roosevelt at the Bowery Branch of the YMCA. Roosevelt, who had recently been named president of the New York City Police Board, a position that was the precursor of police commissioner in our time, was introduced to Raphael, who was hailed as a local hero responsible for saving many women and children from a dangerous fire.

In the biography *Theodore Roosevelt: A Life*, it is reported that Roosevelt was very impressed with Raphael and described their initial meeting this way:

> Occasionally I would myself pick out a man and tell him to take the [police] examination. Thus one evening I went down to speak in the Bowery at the Young Men's Institute, a branch of the Young Men's Christian Association, at the request of Mr. Cleveland H. Dodge. While there he told me he wished to show me a young Jew who had recently, by an exhibition of marked prowess, saved some women and children from a burning building.

> The young Jew, whose name was Otto Raphael, was brought up to see me; a powerful fellow, with good-humored, intelligent face. I asked him about his education, and told him to try the examination [to be a policeman]. He did, passed, was appointed, and made an admirable officer; and he and all his family, wherever they may dwell, have been close friends of mine ever since.

> Otto Raphael was a genuine East Sider. He and I were both "straight New York," to use the vernacular of our native city . . . Otto's parents had come over from Russia, and not only in social standing but in pay a policeman's position meant everything to him. It enabled Otto to educate his little broth-

ers and sisters who had been born in this country, and to bring over from Russia two or three kinsfolk who had perforce been left behind (p. 92).

What Roosevelt does not mention is that Raphael received the highest score of all the police applicants on the physical exam and ranked tenth on the mental exam. As a result of his high scores, he was selected to be one of 85 new recruits from an applicant pool of almost 400 people.

Roosevelt and Raphael became lifelong friends. The future President of the United States also wrote in his autobiography that he admired Raphael as a man of "strong physique and resolute temper, sober, self-respecting, self-reliance, with a strong will to improve himself." Later on, the tall and strong Otto taught Roosevelt how to box and actually became his sparring partner. Subsequently, he would say the traditional Jewish prayer for the dead over Roosevelt's body the night before he was buried.

When Raphael himself died in 1937, he was buried in Brooklyn's Washington Cemetery. Two years later, Theodore Roosevelt, Jr. arranged to have a plaque attached to Raphael's tombstone which read: "Lieutenant Otto Raphael. Who has done credit to the uniform he wore – Theodore Roosevelt."

Simon Eisdorfer

Simon Eisdorfer was born on the Lower East Side on June 14, 1917. He earned a bachelor's degree in chemistry from City College in 1939 with the intention of becoming a chemist. Discovering that he could make a lot more money as a policeman than as a chemist, he joined the police department in 1942. Following service in the U.S. Army during World War II, he returned to the department in 1945.

In the summer of 1972, Eisdorfer, an Assistant Chief Inspector at the New York Police Department, watched as a hostage drama unfolded on TV. What became known as the "Munich massacre" occurred at the 1972 Summer Olympics in Munich Germany, when members of

the Israeli Olympic team were taken hostage by the Palestinian terrorist organization Black September – a group within Yasser Arafat's
Fatah organization. The attack, miserable and failed attempts at negotiations, and botched rescue attempt, eventually led to the deaths of
11 Israeli athletes and one German police officer.

According to news sources, the Israeli athletes had enjoyed a night
out on September 4, 1972, watching a performance of *Fiddler on the
Roof* before returning to the Olympic Village. At 4:30 a.m. on September 5th, as the athletes slept, eight terrorists clad in tracksuits and
carrying guns and grenades in duffel bags, scaled a chain-link fence
with the help of unsuspecting American athletes who, too, were sneak-
ing into the Olympic Village compound. The Palestinians then used
stolen keys to enter two apartments being used by the Israeli team.

Israeli wrestling referee Yossef Gutfreund heard a faint scratching
noise at the door of the first apartment. When he investigated, he saw
the door begin to open and masked men with guns on the other side.
He shouted "Hevre tistalku!" (Guys, get out of here!) and threw his
nearly 300-pound weight against the door to try to stop the Palestinians from forcing their way in. The wrestling coach Moshe Weinberg,
age 33 attacked the kidnappers as the hostages were being moved
from one apartment to another, allowing one of his wrestlers, Gad
Tsobari, to escape. The burly Weinberg knocked one of the intruders
unconscious and stabbed another with a fruit knife before being shot
to death. Weightlifter Yossef Romano, 31 and the father of three ,
also attacked and wounded one of the intruders before being killed.

The kidnappers were left with nine living hostages: wrestling referee
Yossef Gutfreund, age 40; American-born weightlifter David Berger,
28; wrestler Mark Slavin, 18; weightlifting judge Yacov Springer, 51;
weightlifter Ze'ev Friedman, 28; track coach Amitzur Shapira, 40;
wrestler Eliezer Halfin, 24; shooting coach Kehat Shorr, 53; and fencing
coach Andre Spitzer, 27.

The terrorists demanded the release and safe passage to Egypt of
234 Palestinians and non-Arabs jailed in Israel. The German authorities, under the leadership of Chancellor Willy Brandt and Minister

for the Interior Hans-Dietrich Genscher rejected Israel's offer to send an Israeli special forces unit to Germany. Instead, a small squad of German police was dispatched to the Olympic village. Dressed in Olympic sweatsuits and carrying machine guns, these were members of the German border-police, untrained in any sort of counter-terrorist response, and without specific tactics in place for the rescue. The police took up positions and awaited orders which never came.

In the meantime, camera crews filmed the police actions from German apartments, and broadcast the images live to television. With televisions on, the terrorists were able to watch the police as they prepared to attack. Footage shows the terrorists leaning over to look at the police who were in hiding on the roof. In the end, the police simply left.

At one point during the crisis, the negotiators demanded direct contact with the hostages in order to satisfy themselves that the Israelis were still alive. Fencing coach Andre Spitzer, who spoke fluent German, and shooting coach Kehat Shorr, the senior member of the Israeli delegation, had a brief conversation with Schreiber and Genscher while standing at the second-floor window of the besieged building, with two kidnappers holding guns on them. When the kidnappers became impatient with Spitzer's prolonged answers to the negotiators' questions, the coach was pistol-whipped in full view of international television cameras and pulled away from the window.

The kidnappers demanded transportation to Cairo. The German authorities feigned agreement and at 10:10 p.m. two helicopters transported both the kidnappers and their hostages to nearby Fürstenfeldbruck airbase, where a Boeing 727 aircraft was waiting. The kidnappers believed they were on their way to Riem, the international airport near Munich but the authorities planned an assault on the kidnappers at the airport.

Five German snipers, none of whom had any special training, were chosen to shoot the kidnappers. All had been chosen simply because they "shot competitively on weekends." No tanks or armored personnel carriers were at the scene. A Boeing 727 jet was positioned on the tarmac with five or six armed German police inside, who volunteered to do the job, dressed as the flight crew. The plan was for them to overpower the terrorists with the pretense of inspecting the plane, and give the German snipers a chance to kill the terrorists remaining at the helicopters. But they were ordinary police officers who had not been trained for such a mission. At the last minute, as the helicopters were arriving on the tarmac, the German police aboard the airplane voted on and then abandoned their mission, without contact to or from any central command.

The helicopters landed just after 10:30 p.m., and the four pilots and six of the kidnappers emerged. While four of the Black September members held the pilots at gunpoint, Issa and Tony walked over to inspect the jet, only to find it empty. Knowing they had been duped, they jogged hastily back toward the helicopters, and at approximately 11:00 p.m., the German authorities gave the order to the police snipers positioned nearby to open fire.

There was instant chaos. The four German members of the chopper crews began sprinting for safety in all directions. In the ensuing frenzy, two kidnappers standing near the pilots were killed, and a third was mortally wounded as he fled the scene. The three remaining exposed kidnappers scrambled to safety, and began to return fire and shoot out as many airport lights as they could from behind the helicopters, out of the snipers' line of sight. A German policeman in the control tower, Anton Fliegerbauer, was killed by the gunfire. The helicopter pilots fled, but the hostages, who were tied up inside the craft, could not. A stalemate developed. During the gun battle, wrote Groussard, the hostages secretly worked on loosening their bonds. Teeth marks, evidence of the hostages' determination, were found on some of the ropes after the gunfire had ended.

The five German snipers did not have radio contact with each other and were unable to coordinate their fire. None of the snipers were equipped with steel helmets or bullet proof vests, proving an egregious lack of preparation. None of the rifles were equipped with telescopic sights or night-vision scopes. Later it was discovered that one of the snipers never fired a shot because he was positioned directly in the line of friendly fire, without any protective gear. Later in the battle, when kidnapper Khalid Jawad attempted to escape on foot, this sniper shot and killed the fleeing kidnapper, and was in turn wounded by one of his fellow policemen, who was unaware that he was shooting at one of his own men.

At four minutes past midnight, by now into September 6th, one of the kidnappers jumped out of one of the helicopters. He turned and sprayed the helicopter and hostages within with gunfire, killing Springer, Halfin, and Friedman, and wounding Berger in the leg. The kidnapper then pulled the pin on a grenade and tossed it back into the cockpit, where it detonated. While the first helicopter was burning, the surviving kidnappers kept fire trucks at bay by shooting at them.

What happened to the remaining hostages is still a matter of dispute. However, a *Time Magazine* reconstruction of the long-suppressed Bavarian prosecutor's report indicates that a third kidnapper (identified as Adnan Al-Gashey) stood at the door of the helicopter and riddled the remaining five hostages—Gutfreund, Shorr, Slavin, Spitzer and Shapira—with fatal gunfire.

Jim McKay, who was covering the Olympics that year for ABC, had taken on the job of reporting the events as Roone Arledge fed them into his earpiece. After the botched rescue attempt, he came on the air with this statement: "Our worst fears have been realized tonight. They've now said that there were 11 hostages; 2 were killed in their rooms yesterday morning, 9 were killed at the airport tonight. They're all gone."

Almost beyond comprehension, the massacre of 11 Israeli athletes was not considered sufficiently serious to merit canceling or postponing the Olympics. "Incredibly, they're going on with it," Jim Murray of the *Los Angeles Times* wrote at the time. "It's almost like having a dance at Dachau" (September, 1972).

A little over a month later, on October 29th, a Lufthansa jet was hijacked by terrorists demanding that the Munich killers be released. The Germans capitulated and the terrorists were let go, but an Israeli assassination squad was assigned to track them down along with those responsible for planning the massacre. According to George Jonas in *Vengeance: The True Story of an Israeli Counter-Terrorist Team*, eight of the eleven men targeted for death were killed. Of the remaining three, one died of natural causes and the other two were assassinated, but it is not known for sure if they were killed by Israeli agents.

Many counterterrorism experts have theorized that the Munich massacre was one of the most significant terror attacks of recent times, one that set the tone for decades of conflict in the Middle East, and launched a new era of international terrorism.

As the commanding officer of the NYPD's Special Operations division, Eisdorfer realized that such an event could actually happen in New York City. He also knew that the police department was not prepared to deal with it. Accordingly, he developed the operational plans for the nation's first Hostage Negotiation Team. The team became reality in the spring of 1973, months after a high-profile standoff in January in which armed robbers seized a dozen hostages at a Brooklyn sporting goods store and one police officer was killed.

Eisdorfer knew that by putting fresh cops into a hostage situation he could wear down hostage takers. He realized that negotiators could subtly turn a siege into a waiting game that played out in their favor. Police officers could change shifts but the suspects could not, and would become tired and hungry and more likely to surrender. His emphasis was saving lives, not ending things quickly as had unfortunately, and tragically, been done in the past. His techniques worked and would be studied and emulated by police departments all over the world.

Based on Eisdorfer's pioneering work, a special hostage negotiations team is now a permanent fixture of the police department and in incorporated within the Emergency Service Unit (ESU).

The ESU is considered very elite. It is said that when someone needs help they call the police, when the police need help, they call the ESU. The unit provides specialized equipment, expertise and support to the various units within the NYPD. From auto accidents to building collapses to hostage situations, the ESU is called in when the situation requires advanced equipment and expertise.

Also included within the ESU is what is commonly referred to in other agencies as the "SWAT" team. For possible hostage situation, on-scene psychologists and trained police negotiators profile hostage-takers, determine their motivation, vulnerabilities, and dangerousness, suggest dialogue strategies or psychological tactics which would defuse the situation, and spend equal time analyzing which hostages might engage in behaviors that diminish or enhance their chances for survival. A trained hostage negotiator will be able to advise police on whether a hostage taker might be mentally ill (about 50% of them are) and what the extent of their life crisis might be. This is particularly important since some hostage-takers may be out of touch with reality or even attempting to commit "suicide by cop."

In contrast to Eisdorfer's time, crisis / hostage teams now usually consist of at least five people. These include the primary negotiator (who does most of the active negotiations), a secondary negotiator (who monitors negotiations and makes suggestions), an intelligence officer (who seeks and organizes incoming information), a psychologist (who serves as a consultant or advisor), and a tactical liaison (who maintains communications with command)

The first 15 to 45 minutes of a hostage situation are the most dangerous. This is because the hostage-takers are still going through a panic reaction. This is when most hostages get injured or killed, either because they tried to be a hero, made some remark or suggestion, stood out in some symbolic way, or were just picked at random to make a point. Unless the hostage-takers are under the influence of some chemical stimulant, they are likely to calm down after awhile, appear to be exhausted, and tell everyone to get some rest. Hostages may be traded for food, drink, and / or toilet facilities, and these released hostages will be interviewed for what they observed (i.e., numbers of hostage-takers, weapons present, routine, chain of command). Sleep may occur, and this is not uncommon, especially when there is a small number of perpetrators or a solo suspect who has had to handle all the details alone. Authorities use surveillance devices to tell when everyone falls asleep, and have at times surprised everyone by ending a hostage situation during this time.

Felicia Shpritzer

Felicia Shpritzer was born in 1913 to Polish-Jewish parents in Gloversville, New York. She was one of three children. Her parents were in the retail business. As a young girl Shpritzer was instructed in moral values by her family and the importance of hard work and determination. The family eventually moved to New York City to open up a women's apparel shop and Shpritzer attended Hunter College graduating with a degree in mathematics. She attended graduate school at the University of Michigan and at John Jay College of Criminal Justice in police science.

In 1941, Shpritzer joined the New York City Police Department as a policewoman and worked on cases involving the safety and quality of life for women and children. Patrolling in pairs, policewomen worked in movie theatres, parks, zoos and beaches. She worked undercover in vice, prostitution, and abortion cases. Later she was assigned to the police department's Youth Division where she investigated crimes committed against and by juveniles. She loved working with young people, often helping then to get their lives back on track after periods of trouble or bouts with crime.

Beginning in 1892, women who worked in the New York Police Department were hired as "matrons." The matron's uniform, in keeping with the Victorian times, consisted of a long skirt, buttoned-up shirt, and a corset. The job of a matron was to monitor and deal with female detainees and prisoners. Prior to matrons being installed as part of the police department, female arrestees were searched by male officers, their wives, or the maid on duty at the precinct house.

The qualifications for being hired as a police matron originally included being recommended in writing by at least twenty women of "good standing," and passing a civil-service test. The job was hard, the hours were long, and there was only one day off each month. A matron's pay as of 1917 was $1,000 a year. But 1918 became an auspicious year for the matrons as they received their first raise and were at times permitted to actually supervise male officers in certain situations. That same year, the NYPD appointed its first six official "policewomen," who each earned a salary of $1,200 a year.

Titles and job duties continued to change, and by 1937 all women on the police department were called policewomen. In addition to the titles and pay, policewomen's uniforms changed as well. In 1937 they were permitted to wear knee-length skirts, heels and gloves. In 1943, Mayor Fiorello La Guardia (himself half Jewish) issued the first combination gun and makeup bag. The mayor told the policewomen: "Use your gun as you would your lipstick—use it only when you need it, use it intelligently, and don't overdo either one."

In 1961, when the New York City Police Department refused to allow Shpritzer to take the sergeant's exam, she took the matter to court under a theory of discrimination. Police Commissioner Michael J. Murphy opposed her suit, submitting an affidavit in which he declared that women lacked the physical strength and endurance required of a police sergeant. He also pointed to a section of the code that read, "There shall only be one rank of policewomen within the Police Department." But Shpritzer cited a section of the City Administrative Code providing that any member of the Police Department assigned to the Juvenile Aid Bureau (where she worked) "shall retain his or her rank and pay in the force and shall be eligible for promotion as if serving in the uniformed forces." Accordingly, she asserted, she should not be barred from taking the promotional exam.

Following a long legal battle, in 1964 the New York State Court of Appeals (New York State's highest court) upheld Shpritzer's right to take the Sergeant's promotional exam as well as other promotional exams.

By winning this landmark case Shpritzer opened up the ranks to women in the NYPD, and one year later 125 policewomen also took the Sergeant's exam. The case also set a legal precedent for female officers across America to take promotional exams and to seek advancement.

But this success did not come without a price. Shpritzer was resented by many of her peers, including many women who feared that their work details were being jeopardized and that their comfortable routines in the police department might be disturbed. They wrote discouraging and even threatening letters, some of which actually appeared in local Civil Service newspapers, in the "letters to the editor" column.

Undaunted, Shpritzer went on to take the Lieutenant's and Captain's exams and was subsequently promoted to Lieutenant and assigned to the 9th Precinct in one of the city's toughest neighborhoods.

Her good friend detective Kathy Burke recalls the first time she met Shpritzer in 1968. She was wearing a trench coat and loafers, and carrying two shopping bags. "Oh darling, you look so good," she would blurt out effusively in her thick Yiddish accent. "She looked and acted like the typical Jewish mother" recalls Burke. She was in the habit of bringing homemade chicken soup to the officers in her command, and always lamented that they looked too thin. Like the teacher that she was, "she used to grade our police reports with a red pencil checking for grammar and punctuation" adds Burke. Like any Jewish mother, she comforted her subordinates when they had problems, and scolded them when they were wrong (K. Burke, personal communication, November 15, 2005).

In 1976 Shpritzer was on the promotional list for Captain, but she turned 63 that year and had to retire pursuant to law. She appealed this rule and the decision was relegated to Police Commissioner Michael Codd who decided against her. Shpritzer retired from the police department in 1976 as a lieutenant.

Gertrude Schimmel

Deputy Chief Gertrude D. T. Schimmel, the second highest ranking woman ever in the New York City Police Department, began her career as a policewoman on June 5, 1940.

Schimmel was born in the Bronx in 1918. She received a good Jewish education and attended "Talmud Torah" as a young girl. She graduated from Hunter College in 1939 and did very well (she was Phi Beta Kappa). Her family thought it was strange that she would want to enter police work but understood that, aside from teaching, this was the job that paid the most. So she became part of the famous police academy "class of 1940" which included an inordinately large and unprecedented number of college-educated Jews. As women, "we didn't box or do the two-mile run" says Schimmel, but other than that, the police academy training for women was the same as for men (G. Schimmel, personal communication, December 10, 2005).

During the early years on the job she was assigned to the Bureau of Policewomen where she performed a wide variety of duties including many special investigations for the Police Commissioner's Office and the Chief Inspector (now the Chief of Patrol). She was also assigned to the Juvenile Aid Bureau (now the Youth Division) working with young people in trouble. She had always been interested in young people and enjoyed helping and advising them. In 1960 she even wrote a book called *Joan Palmer, Policeman*, which was published by Dodd, Mead and did fairly well.

Her book outlined the experiences of a fictional newly hired policewoman named Joan Palmer, and was based on her own experiences as a policewoman.

Many of the events and descriptions depicted in the book reveal how women on the force were perceived in the 1940s and seem almost ancient by today's standards. To begin with, policewomen, due to their sex were not "police officers" or "patrolmen" but rather something quite different. The basic job of a patrolman was to patrol a beat in uniform. The job of a policewoman usually involved working in civilian clothes. They would work with juveniles, look for pick pockets, and act as decoys (such as in prostitution cases).

Policewomen were referred to as "girls" in those days, and everyone seemed to know that one of their primary reasons for taking the job in the first place was to find a husband. "Most of the girls who come on single end up marrying policemen" said a fictional supervisor in the book. But there were exceptions, for example, the same supervisor revealed that she did not marry a policeman but rather a lawyer who she met on a court case. "So I think the Police Department should get credit for my marriage, too" she claimed (p. 15).

In her book, Schimmel's account of her policewoman's class meeting the Mayor of the City of New York would make a current-day sexual harassment lawyer cringe. "My girls," began the Mayor, "yes, you are my girls . . . with the new look, and I feel a little bit like Pygmalion, because I created you. In the old days, a policewoman was a heavy-weight. Under my administration, that has all changed. You're young, smart and streamlined . . . now try to keep that girlish figure" (p. 19).

Fortunately, Policewoman Schimmel was not satisfied with being one of the Mayor's girls, or in simply keeping her girlish figure. She wanted to be a full-fledged police officer and not a second class citizen. She also wanted the opportunity to become a supervisor on equal par with male supervisors on the force.

In 1965, along with Felicia Shpritzer, Schimmel, became one of the first two female sergeants in the NYPD. Accepting this change in status for women on the department, Commissioner Michael Murphy (successor to Patrick Murphy) called the appointment "a significant milestone in [the] department's history." In that rank, Schimmel served as a supervisor in the Bureau of Policewomen, and later as a confidential aid to the Chief Inspector. Promoted to Lieutenant on December 19, 1967 (another first), she was assigned as Commanding Officer of the "Know Your Police Department" program which was an information and community relations program for school children.

On August 26, 1971 she was sworn in as the police department's first woman Captain by Mayor John Lindsay in a City Hall ceremony. As a Captain in charge of the Policewomen's Section, she laid the ground-work for the first experiment with policewomen on patrol, a program which proved successful and was eventually extended citywide.

But not all women on the department were anxious to jump into radio cars and patrol the streets. Those who were investigators pre-ferred to keep things as they were rather than give up the comfort of a nice desk job in a squad room for the action (and danger) of the road. In fact, when the call came out for women to work patrol, all the women detectives said "no" but all the uniformed policewomen said "yes."

For Schimmel, the greatest victories for women in the NYPD came in 1973 when all policewomen officially became "police officers." Along with this came equality in the ranks, and women took the same test, gained the same title, wore the same uniform and shield and took the same assignments. Gone were the skirts and bags of the old days. Female police officers now wore pants and gun belts like male officers and the days of the policewoman were forever gone.

Schimmel served on the police department during some of it's most turbulent and difficult times. This included the investigations and hearings of the Knapp Commission into police corruption and money-taking. "I was for the Knapp Commission" recalls Schimmel, who was steadfastly against the taking of bribes or any unethical behavior on the part of the police. She was aware that police officers were openly accepting money, "Christmas time they even had a list" she recalls (G. Schimmel, personal communication, December 10, 2005).

During her time on the department Schimmel held many official jobs and ranks. But she also held many "unofficial" jobs such as speech writer for Police Commissioner Codd and at times for Mayor Beam as well. She was also asked several times by the Police Commissioner to go to the police academy and give pep talks to the women recruits to prevent them from getting frustrated and resigning. One of the things she discussed in these pep talks was the unlimited work possibilities in the police department, and how as a police officer, you are afforded a "front row seat on life" which allows you to see things that most people could only imagine.

In 1978, Schimmel made history with her appointment to the rank of deputy chief. This was the highest rank ever attained by any female officer at that time – not to mention a Jewish one. She recommends police work for Jewish men and women as an excellent means of public service. She retired from the department in 1981 after more than 41years performing her own public service.

Al Seedman

From 1971-1972, Al Seedman was in charge of the largest municipal detective bureau in the world. In fact, with 3,300 detectives, the detective bureau was larger than most police departments and even the entire

Federal Bureau of Investigation at the time. Perhaps this is why J. Edgar Hoover called Seedman personally to insure him of the bureau's complete cooperation in sharing information on important cases.

Seedman grew up poor in the Bronx where his father worked as a cab driver. He attended Baruch School of Business with the intention of becoming an accountant but found that he could not be hired by many firms due the intense anti-Semitism which existed at the time. As was the case with most Jewish men who took the police exam in 1939, it was financial security and a steady paycheck which was on his mind and not the idea of being a crime-fighter, and he soon discovered that he could make more money as a police officer than as an accountant. But there was another reason which led Seedman into police work, and in his 1971 book *Chief!* he addresses this.

> *Whenever I was running a big case, reporters would ask me the same damn question: "When did you decide you wanted to be a cop?" I would tell them I got sold on the career as a kid when they made me an official Stairwell Monitor at P.S. 93 in the Bronx. The reporters would always snicker. They thought I was being sarcastic. I let them think what they pleased. But I really **did** love being a Stairwell Monitor – not because it gave me a chance to boss other kids around, but because it made me feel good to see things happen right, with order and authority* (Seedman, 1971, p. 27).

The idea of being a cop – or wearing any kind of uniform did not set well with Seedman's mother, she did not think this was right for a Jewish boy. In his book he describes her reaction.

> *Then one day when I was a sophomore at Townsend Harris, I told [my mother] I was considering applying to West Point or Annapolis. She went through the roof. No son of her was voluntarily going to put on a uniform. Part of her reaction*

was a mother's natural belief that to wear a uniform meant to risk getting wounded. But it was also a gut response, a Jew's traditional aversion to the uniform, any uniform. In the Old Country, Jews were not allowed to join the Army; so the only uniforms they saw belonged to the Cossacks who galloped through their Shtetls (Seedman, 1971, p. 25).

This graduating class of the 1940 police academy was composed of an inordinately large number of Jewish men with college degrees. This represented the dawning of a new age for the NYPD. Before this, the ranks of the force were composed mostly of blue-collar Irish and Italian cops without a college education who came from families of cops going back for generations. It was these generational and cultural ties to the police department which gave them their chances for promotion. But all this changed in 1940 with the "Jewish academy class" of college-educated men who entered the ranks of the department. As Seedman states, "the Irish and Italians did not have a chance" (A. Seedman, personal communication, November 12, 2005).

When he was Chief of Detectives Seedman worked out of a suite of offices located on the second floor of police headquarters. He had a staff of about 20, all detectives. A captain sat in the outer room of Seedman's personal office and served as his executive secretary. This captain would control who got access to the chief.

In his book *Target Blue*, Robert Daley described Seedman as an impressive and well-dressed figure.

His suits were always the latest style and he wore big knot ties and monogrammed shirts. The name "Al" was always embroidered on his cuffs in script. He also wore a great deal of jewelry. He had a number of watches, some of them encrusted with diamonds, and he wore rings on both hands, sometimes changing them from day to day. His cuff links also changed from day to day. Some of these cuff links were miniature Chief of Detectives shields and others were solid gold. He

owned a number of .38-caliber revolvers, including a smoothly
polished hammerless model which looked like a work of jewelry.
He sometimes wore this gun or another one in a suede holster,
but he also had many of his suits made with pistol-shaped
pockets sewn into the lining (Seedman, 1971, p. 249).

Seedman gave a somewhat stocky appearance even though was only
about 185 pounds. He almost always had a Cuban cigar stuck in his
mouth and tended to growl his words without removing the cigar. He
looked tough, and he was tough. He also never smiled. Because of
all this, he was known as "Big Al," "Smiley," or "Mr. Cigar."

Sometimes Seedman's toughness got him in trouble. As a captain
in 1962, he was standing with a man named Anthony Dellernia, who
with his partner had murdered two detectives but now refused to
pose for photographers. Seedman had grabbed the guy's hair and jerked
his head back, exposing the murderer's face to the world. The resulting photo was highly dramatic especially with the cigar clenched
between Seedman's teeth. The New York Civil Liberties Union
demanded that he be reprimanded for abusing the prisoner and, although
no action was ever taken, Seedman never again allowed himself to
be photographed with a cigar in his mouth.

In his book *Chief!*, he talks about how he had a reputation for always
taking over a new command just as the most memorable cases were
about to break.

Soon after he was appointed a captain and Commander of Brooklyn's 10th District in 1962, a double murder of two detectives took
place. It was May 18, 1962 and the call came out as a "10-30" or
felony in progress. But immediately upon entering the Borough Park
Tobacco store at 1167 48th Street in Borough Park, he knew something much more sinister had taken place. Inside the store and lying
dead on the floor were two police detectives by the names of Luke
Fallon and John Finnegan who were gunned down in their attempts
to foil an armed robbery of the store. It would be Seedman and his

team of detectives who would later solve the case.

Two years after the Fallon-Finnegan murders, in the 17th District in Queens Seedman was thrust into the Kitty Genovese murder case which turned out to be one of the most famous in the city's history. Seedman described the case in *Chief!*

Catherine (or "Kitty" as she was sometimes called) was an attractive, outgoing young woman who moved to the Kew Gardens section of Queens in 1963. She worked as a bar manager in Ev's Eleventh Hour Club, a small neighborhood tavern on Jamaica Avenue and 193rd Street in the Hollis section of the borough. The bar was about five miles from her apartment, and she drove her red Fiat to the restaurant nearly every night. She worked late, sometimes into the early morning hours.

On March 13, 1964, in the early morning hours, Catherine left work and parked her car in the Long Island Railroad parking lot which was located about twenty feet from her apartment door at 82-70 Austin Street. As she locked her car door she noticed a man in the darkness walking towards her. She became anxious as the man began to follow her. "As she got out of the car she saw me and ran," the man told the court later, "I ran after her and I had a knife in my hand."

She must have thought that since the entrance to her building was so close, she would reach safety within seconds. But the man was faster than she thought. He caught up with Catherine near a street light at the end of the parking lot. "I could run much faster than she could, and I jumped on her back and stabbed her several times," the man later told detectives (Seedman, 1971, p. 127).

"Oh my God! He stabbed me!" she screamed. "Please help me! Please help me!" Some apartment lights went on in nearby buildings. One woman at 82-68 Austin Street heard Catherine's screams plainly. "There was another shriek," she later testified in court, "and she was lying down crying out." Up on the seventh floor of the same building, a resident slid open his window and observed the struggle below. "Hey, let that girl alone!" he yelled down into the street. The attacker heard him and immediately walked away. There was quiet once again in the dark. The only sound was Catherine sobbing, struggling to her feet. Bleeding badly from several stab wounds, Catherine managed to reach the side of her building and held onto the concrete wall. She staggered over to a locked door and tried to stay conscious. Within five minutes, the assailant returned. He stabbed her again (Seedman, 1971, p. 113).

"I'm dying! I'm dying!" she cried. Several people in her building heard her screams. Lights went on once again and some windows opened. Tenants tried to see what was happening from the safety of their apartments. The attacker then ran to a white Chevy Corvair at the edge of the railroad parking lot and seemed to drive away. On the sixth floor of 82-40 Austin Street, a couple of residents witnessed the attack from their window. "I saw a man hurry to a car under my window," the witness said later. "He left and came back five minutes later and was looking around the area." The witness wanted to call the police, but his wife would not let him. "I didn't let him," she later said to the press. "I told him there must have been 30 calls already." A young woman who lived on the second floor heard the commotion from her window. "I heard a scream for help, three times, "she later told the court, "I saw a girl lying down on the pavement with a man bending down over her, beating her" (Seedman, 1971, p. 114).

At about 3:25 a.m., Catherine, bleeding badly, stumbled to the rear of her apartment building and attempted to enter through a back entrance but the door was locked. She slid along the wall until she reached a hallway leading to the 2nd floor of 82-62 Austin Street but she fell to the vestibule floor. In the meantime, the man had returned again. "I came back because I knew I'd not finished what I set out to do," he told cops later. He followed the trail of blood to the doorway where Catherine lay bleeding on the tiled floor. And there he sexually assaulted and killed her.

About a week after the murder, detectives located a milkman who was able to furnish a description of a suspect. But it wasn't until six days later, when a suspect was arrested stealing a television during a house burglary that detectives made an arrest: Winston Moseley, age 29.

Moseley had no criminal record. He was married, owned a home in Queens and had two kids. Soon after his arrest he told detectives of two other murders he had committed, Barbara Kralik, 15 year old, on July 20 in Springfield Gardens, Queens, and Annie Mae Johnson, 24 years old, of South Ozone Park, Queens, on February 29.

After his conviction, Moseley was remanded to the Department of Corrections and eventually sent to Attica prison. In 1967, the New York State Court of Appeals found that evidence of Moseley's mental condition should have been admitted into trial, and his death sentence was reduced to life imprisonment. In 1968, during a routine transfer to a hospital in Buffalo, Moseley managed to overpower a guard and steal his gun. He later took five people hostage and raped a woman in front of her husband. The FBI located the escaped killer in a second floor apartment in downtown Buffalo. An FBI agent named Neil Welch managed to enter the apartment and for a nail-biting half hour, Moseley and Welch pointed guns at each other point-blank while they continued negotiations. Moseley later surrendered.

During the period of 1984 through 2006, Moseley appeared before the state parole board seven times without success.

When the Kitty Genovese story appeared in the newspaper, the public was outraged. How could people be so insensitive to the suffering of another? Why didn't anyone help her? Some newspaper editors and psychiatrists at the time blamed this behavior on "bystander apathy," "lack of altruism," or growing "urban alienation."

"Altruism" is the extent to which one believes that people are basically unselfish and sincerely interested in others. The witnessed murder of Kitty Genovese forced New Yorkers and Americans as a whole to reevaluate their basic beliefs about the extent of altruism in human nature.

The incident led to a research program by social psychologists John Darley and Bibb Latane, who found that one reason why individuals fail to act was because of an awareness that a large number of other people are also watching. They referred to this phenomenon as a "diffusion of responsibility."

One of Latane and Darley's studies dealt with responses to the victim of a fall. It was found that if the observers of the accident were strangers to one another, they were less likely to aid the victim than if they had been prior acquaintances. Other situational factors were also important. If a person had just observed another person perform a helpful act, he himself was likely to act in a helpful manner as well. When mixed racial groups observed a victim in difficulty, there was some tendency for observers of the same race as the victim to offer help more than for observers of another race to do so. Population differences also appeared to be important in willingness to help. People in urban areas were less likely to help than those from smaller towns or rural areas.

In another study, Latane and Darley created an "emergency" by having the room in which subjects were completing written surveys gradually fill with smoke. In another experiment, subjects heard a loud crashing noise from an adjoining room, followed by a woman's screaming, "Oh my God, my foot . . . I . . . I . . . can't move it. Oh my ankle. I . . . can't get this . . . thing off me." In yet another study, subjects were participating in a discussion over an intercom when one of them suddenly choked, gasped, and called out for help (Latane and Darley, 1970, p. 13).

In each of these studies, the number of individuals present at the time of the emergency was varied so that some subjects were alone and others were with several people. The researchers consistently found that as the number of bystanders increased, the likelihood that any one of them would help decreased. It appeared that people help others more often and more quickly when alone. This phenomenon, which is often called the "bystander effect" or a "norm of inaction," has been explained from a psychological point of view.

First, the more bystanders present, the more likely it is that people will assume someone else will help. If someone is with just one other person when an emergency occurs, the observer or bystander perceives that he is 100% responsible for taking action. However, when there are 10 bystanders, each perceives himself to have only a tenth of the responsibility. The higher the number of bystanders, the less obligated each individual is likely to feel to intervene.

Second, if someone is unsure of his own perceptions and interpretations, or if the situation is ambiguous, he looks to others for help in defining what is going on. If others appear calm, he may decide that whatever is happening doesn't require any assistance.

Unfortunately, people often try to avoid showing outward signs of worry or concern until they see that other people are alarmed. This sort of caution encourages others not to define the situation as one requiring assistance, and therefore inhibits the urge to help. The larger the number of people who don't seem concerned, the stronger the inhibiting influence.

Kitty Genovese's neighbors weren't necessarily cruel, cold, or apathetic. They may simply have been victims of social influence, with each looking to others for information, waiting for someone else to define the situation and act. Because everyone was waiting for someone else to do something, no one did anything.

Soon after taking command of the Manhattan South Detective Bureau in 1969, Seedman was almost immediately confronted by the bombing campaign of a white revolutionary and anti-war activist named Sam Melville.

Melville was the leader of a group of activists and revolutionaries that also included Jane Alpert. Starting with the detonation on July 26, 1969, of two dynamite bombs on a pier on the Hudson, the group's campaign eventually included eight Manhattan targets and several in other cities. Not one of their many bombs caused a fatality.

The young white revolutionaries, fueled by the increasing stridency of the anti-war and radical movement of the time, and their own conviction that revolution was just around the corner, set to work in a tireless fashion. The U.S. Induction Center on Whitehall Street was taken out, and the group released a flamboyant communiqué - "This action was taken in support of the NLF, legalized marijuana, love, Cuba, legalized abortion, and all the American revolutionaries and GIs who are winning the war against the Pentagon. Nixon, surrender now!"

The group also hit the Marine Midland Bank on Broadway (evidently on a whim of Melville's, who was not a stable character, even for a bomber; justification for the act was concocted after the fact), the Criminal Courts Building at 100 Centre Street, and targets in

Minneapolis, Milwaukee, and Chicago (although this last bomb failed to go off).

Then came the group's major move. On the night of November 11, 1969, bombs when off simultaneously on the 19th floor of the General Motors Building, the 20th floor of the RCA building, and the 16th floor of Chase Manhattan Bank. This stupendous run caused panic throughout the city and precipitated more than 200 bomb threats, but failed to produce the anticipated uprising of the masses.

The very next evening, November 12th, Sam Melville slung a knapsack of bombs over his shoulder and headed out from his building with accomplice George Demmerle. His intention was to place explosives in the Army trucks parked outside the National Guard Armory at Lexington Avenue and 26th Street. The trucks would be driven inside at night and the bombs would be perfectly placed for maximum damage to the state's property. However, George Demmerle turned out to be an FBI informer. Melville's intentions were known all along and he was arrested with his ticking bombs alongside the Armory.

Melville pleaded guilty to Federal bomb conspiracy and state arson charges, and was sentenced to 18 years in prison. In September 1971, he was killed in the Attica Prison uprising along with 31 other prisoners and 11 Hostages. When he was found dead behind a barricade, three homemade bombs lay on the ground just beyond his hand.

Seedman knew a great many rich people, played golf with some of them and handball with others. He knew all about jewelry and all about restaurants. He knew the owners of many fine New York restaurants socially, and when he entered one of these places, he would be sure to get the best table and the best service. He also believed in the good life and kept a small refrigerator in the corner of his office which was stocked with Chivas whiskey.

In 1971, Seedman and Commissioner Patrick Murphy expanded and perfected the Premise Protection Squad which was developed in 1969 as a new approach in fighting crime in New York City. The basic premise of the project was that certain common characteristics made locations or businesses within New York City more likely targets of crime. As a sub unit within the Detective Division's Safe, Loft and Truck Squad, the unit was staffed with personnel who had strong investigative experience and some background, education, or training in the field of physical security.

Now called the Crime Prevention Squad, the unit provided crime prevention services and programs to the citizens and businesses of New York City that included conducting security surveys, lectures, the administration of crime reduction programs and various forms of outreach. These free services not only reduced crime but also reduced the fear and perception of crime by making the citizens and businesses a part of the solution.

Over the course of the next six years (1972-1978) the Section was transferred from the Office of the Chief of Detectives to the Special Operations Division; shortly thereafter, to the Chief of Patrol; and then to the Office of the Deputy Commissioner of Community Affairs. On July 5, 2001, the Office of the Deputy Commissioner was reorganized, and the Crime Prevention Section was placed under the aegis of the Chief of Department. Today the unit has expanded its areas of expertise and services and is still acclaimed as a positive approach to crime reduction.

Seedman's tenure as Chief of Detectives coincided with some of the most dramatic events of New York City and the country. These included The Knapp Commission, the murder of Crazy Joe Gallo, the Kitty Genovese murder, the international narcotics ring which was later depicted in the movie *The French Connection*, the firing of legendary Detective Eddie Egan (played by Gene Hackman in the same movie), the murders of police officers by members of the Black Liberation Army, and much more. But of all the cases he had to handle, the most painful might have been those involving the murder of fellow police officers.

On May 19, 1971, NYPD Officers Thomas Curry and Nicholas Binetti were shot on Riverside Drive in Manhattan. Two nights later, two other officers, Waverly Jones and Joseph Piagentini, were shot and killed in Harlem. In separate messages delivered to the media, the Black Liberation Army claimed responsibility for both attacks.

Immediately after these shootings, the FBI made the investigation of these incidents, called "Newkill," a part of their long-standing program investigating the Black Liberation Army and the Black Panthers. J. Edgar Hoover instructed the New York Office of the FBI to consider the possibility that these attacks may be the result of revenge taken against the police by the Black Panther Party stemming from an earlier arrest of Panther members in another case (the "Panther 32 case").

Hoover met with then President Richard Nixon who told Hoover that he wanted to make sure that the FBI was going all out in gathering information on the situation in New York. "Newkill" became a joint FBI/NYPD operation involving total cooperation and sharing of information. The FBI made all its facilities and resources, including its laboratory, available to the NYPD. In turn, Seedman, who coordinated the NYPD's investigation, ordered his subordinates to give the FBI "all available information developed to date, as well as in future investigations."

On June 5, 1971, Bin Wahad was arrested during a robbery of a Bronx after hours hangout for local drug merchants. Seized from inside the social club was a .45 caliber machine gun. Although there is some controversy whether ballistic tests on the weapon linked it with the Curry-Binetti shooting, Bin Wahad was successfully prosecuted and convicted of the murders.

Soon after the police officer murders came the murder of underworld figure "Crazy" Joe Gallo. Born in Brooklyn, Gallo earned his nickname of "crazy" in mafia circles because his plans for the future of the mob were so unique. He saw the future of organized crime as involving criminal activities in Harlem and other black neighborhoods. Gallo and his brother did some work for Carlo Gambino, and were credited by most sources to be the assassins in Murder Inc.

Gallo was one of the first mafiosi to predict a shift of power in the New York streets from the Italian mafia to black gangs, and he started becoming friends with members of some of these gangs. Gallo was also an alley of Carlo Gambino against Joseph Colombo. Colombo was shot in June 1971 by a black gunman named Jerome

Johnson. Johnson, who was immediately shot dead by Colombo's bodyguards, was believed to be an associate of Gallo and therefore Gallo was widely suspected by both the police and the mob as being the one behind Colombo's shooting.

On April 7, 1972, Gallo was celebrating his 43rd birthday with his family at a restaurant, "Umberto's Clam House " at 129 Mulberry street in Little Italy in New York City, when three gunmen burst in and opened fire. Women screamed. Patrons hit the floor. Gallo got up from the table and ran for the door. He was hit five times and died outside on the sidewalk. The gunmen were never identified or convicted. At his funeral, Gallo's sister cried over his coffin that "The streets are going to run red with blood, Joey!"

If you were to stop a New York City police officer on the beat and ask, "Who is the chief of detectives?" chances are he or she would not know. But Al Seedman was the chief of detectives that *everybody* knew. Even today when he goes to One Police Plaza, they roll out the red carpet. On a recent trip there Commissioner Kelly insisted that Seedman come to his conference room during a major command meeting to meet his staff. When Seedman walked in he was introduced as a "living legend" and rightly so. One of the things he told the assembled group was that even after being retired for over 30 years, there isn't a day that goes by that he does not miss the job. There is also not a day that goes by that he does not carry his solid gold Chief of Detectives badge in his pocket (and gun on his hip). The badge was not department issue but was given to him by the loyal detectives under his command (A. Seedman, personal communication, November 12, 2005).

Looking back on his career, Seedman is particularly proud that he was instrumental in the hiring of one of the police department's most famous rabbis, Alvin Kass. He recalls when then police Commissioner Leary tasked him with this job and how at first he was not particularly impressed with any of the candidates and then "along came this skinny little guy" who made an impression on Seedman and the others on the panel because he was carrying an attaché case which turned out to have racket ball gloves and sneakers in it. These things showed Seedman that Kass was an all right guy.

Seedman recalls how Commissioner Patrick Murphy did not particularly like detectives and pretty much "thought we were all thieves" because we spent so much time in bars and similar establishments. What Murphy did not always understand was that detectives had to gather information in order to make their cases and this was a lot different from what the uniformed guys had to do (A. Seedman, personal communication, November 12, 2005).

In contrast to Commissioner Murphy's perception of detectives, Seedman has always been impressed with their high level of decency and trustworthiness. In his book *Chief!*, he discussed one of his colleagues' honesty.

> Ray McGuire, the captain who had run the squad for years, was famous for his integrity . . . One Friday, just before Christmas in 1947, I helped lug into the safe and loft office dozens of cartons of toys that had been recovered from a hijacking case. There were dolls, teddy bears, [and] stuffed animals of all kinds.

> Ray McGuire, while overseeing the operation, suddenly looked up and saw that it was close to three o'clock. "I'm never going to get to lunch," he said. "I was going to stop by Macy's to pick up some toys for my girls." One of the other detectives mentioned he had to do the same at Macy's. McGuire handed him a twenty-dollar bill. "Pick up a pair of dolls for me, will ya?"

> If there were two dolls in that office, there were two thousand . . . Yet I doubt it ever occurred to McGuire that a pair would never be missed. Or that the owner would be delighted to make them a gift (Seedman, 1971, p. 43).

"Commissioner Kennedy was impressed with me for some reason" is how Seedman describes his entrée into higher-level command. Kennedy was particularly impressed with Seedman's meticulous way of keeping records and attending to in detail in anything that he was asked to do. These qualities landed him the job of teaching at the police academy. Seedman always liked to teach, in fact this was a passion for him. He recalls, for example, how while preparing for the sergeant exam he walked his beat in the middle of the night and practiced aloud things he could teach new cops as a supervisor. Soon Commissioner Murphy gave him the job of writing the complete academic training program for all new recruits at the police academy (A. Seedman, personal communication, November 12, 2005).

Seedman already had a bachelor's degree in accounting upon entering the police department. He later earned a master's degree from John Jay College and a Doctor of Public Administration degree from New York University. Al Seedman is a doctor! Seedman could have remained in an academic path as he was offered the chair of the Criminal Justice department at American University in Washington D.C. but turned it down due to the relatively low pay.

Seedman enjoyed every single moment of his time on the job. He liked being in the center of things and where the action was. He liked the fact that it was the press that called *him* when something big went down in the city. Usually this was a homicide, Al went to over 2,000 of these while he was Chief of Detectives. He was trusted by the commissioner to determine when he had to be notified and when to notify the mayor.

To this day Al carries his gold Chief of Detectives shield in his pocket and his .38 revolver "in case there's trouble." He can remember, "feeling ten feet tall" when he arrived on a crime scene, took that shield out of this pocket, and hung it around his neck.

This greater-than-life persona did not go unnoticed by Hollywood. One television show, *Eischied*, was clearly based on Seedman and he was played by the actor Joe Don Baker. Seedman could not get over how an actor with a southern accent could play a guy from the Bronx.

In the show, Earl Eischied was the rough and "hands-on" Chief of Detectives, who although a firm believer in law and order, was not above bending the law here and there if it got results, much to the chagrin of the fussy Deputy Commissioner Kimbrough. Eischied mostly had a desk job, but would rather be on the streets busting heads than pushing pencils in an office. Earl's pet cat was named "P.C." (for Police Commissioner). Deputy Chief Inspector Ed Parks was played by the real-life Eddie Egan (from the French Connection). Raymond Burr appeared on two episodes as the Police Commissioner and there were guest appearances by many notables such as Jim Backus.

Supposedly the television show Kojak was also based on Seedman except that the cigar was replaced with a lollipop. Kojak had a cynical sense of humor and was determined to do things his way regardless of what his bosses thought. He was outspoken and street-wise, and was not above stretching the literal interpretation of the law if it would help crack a case.

Seedman also had a part in the movie *Report to the Commissioner* where the director wanted him to play the mayor but Al said, "I'm a cop, not a politician." To tell his own story, Seedman wrote a book, *Chief!*, which recounted his 30 years on the police department, including the time of the Knapp Commission hearings. As Chief of Detectives, Seedman was required to assign detectives as body-guards for Frank Serpico. Typically in such situations bodyguards are with their charges 24 hours a day, and even slept in their houses. But Serpico distrusted the police so much that he would not allow them to stay in his apartment. Al recalls, "these guys had to stand outside all night freezing their — off" (A. Seedman, personal communication, November 12, 2005).

David Durk

David Durk grew up in a spacious apartment on West End Avenue in Manhattan. His father was a surgeon and his family had a car, a housekeeper, and definitely no financial worries. He attended an Ivy

League college in Massachusetts where almost all of his classmates were white Anglo-Saxon Protestants with wealthy parents. He was one of the only Jews. Following graduation he entered law school at Columbia and drove a taxicab at night in order to help pay his tuition. But he was not really happy.

With an interest in the "urban crisis" he saw in society, and an eye for politics, he joined the New York City police Department in 1963. He was not the typical police recruit. For one he was a Jew. He also came from a white-collar family of some means. This was much different from the predominantly Irish Catholic, blue-collar world that he was now immersed in.

Durk believed strongly that the police department should do everything it could to attract the brightest and most educated men to be police officers. He was actually awarded a grant by the National Institute for Law Enforcement and Criminal Justice to go to various college campuses and recruit students into police work. He would go to places like Harvard, Yale, Princeton, and NYU and try and convince students that if they really wanted to help people they should become a cop.

Former Deputy Commissioner of the NYPD, Robert Daley, author of *Target Blue*, would accompany Durk on many of his college visits. Hundreds of students at Ivy League colleges would show up to listen to Durk's recruiting message. "If the thought of seeing a problem on the street and doing something about it appeals to you," he once told a group of Harvard undergraduates, "become a cop." "Being a cop is a socially critical job," he would tell the students. He would want to know what they were doing with their lives now. "How do you justify your existence, friend? You only have one life. You say you're interested in true justice? You say you're a liberal? Well this is what liberalism comes down to. What are you contributing to society?"

"It's an absolutely succulent job," Durk would tell his audiences, "I was bored out of my skull. Then I became a cop. I love being a cop. It isn't bank holdups, it's family fights. It's taking pushers and muggers off the street. It's showing compassion when people are in trouble. And it's fun. That siren and those red lights are fun. It's a job where altruism merges with fun."

Scores of college students from schools such as Yale, Harvard, and Amherst, signed up to take the police exam following Durk's motivational speeches. This did not always make their high brow wealthy patents happy. "I send my kid to Yale to become a cop?" asked one incredulous father (D. Durk, personal communication, January 30, 2006).

Some his bosses at the police department were also not so thrilled with his recruitment efforts. Once, returning from a college trip, he went to police headquarters to file his report. A deputy inspector in personnel said to him "Durk, why do we want all those college kids coming here looking for jobs? They will only be troublemakers."

Sometimes his greetings on college campuses were also not so sweet. In 1971 he was supposed to give a talk at the UCLA at Berkeley's Center for Law and Social Policy. At the last minute, the university cancelled his talk because radical students had threatened to burn down the building if he spoke there. He mused at the time how he was regarded by many in the New York City Police Department as a radical troublemaker, and by the Berkeley students as an establishment pig. He couldn't win.

Durk felt that the key to the future of the police department was in hiring good people with motivation. He did not see this happening, and he absolutely made no bones about telling anyone who would listen about it. He felt that the department was hiring incompetent, lazy, and undereducated people who quickly learned from the older cops how to be even lazier and more incompetent.

"Motivation is the key" he said. And the department should have the highest of standards. "The Foreign Legion" has greater standards than the police department (D. Durk, personal communication, January 30, 2006).

Durk had always been convinced that a new breed of committed cops could radically change the quality of U.S. law enforcement. In a 1970 interview with *TIME* Magazine, he suggested that too many officers are insensitive to the needs of the ghetto. "We need policemen who worry about the kid getting raped on the tenement roof, not those who look out of the window of their patrol car and say 'See the animals.' We need more cops who care to identify with the people they are supposed to protect."

Making a science of sizing up individual cops, Durk found a lot of great ones on the department. Although almost none of the cops he observed had his kind of formal education, they had a sense of street smarts which he admired.

He came to the conclusion that most cops had joined the police department for altruistic reasons, although not many of them would admit it. Although most of them wanted to do the right thing, they did not feel supported by their superiors or by the system, and after a couple of years on the job would become cynical, frustrated, and open to corruption. Durk felt that about 10 percent of the police force was corrupt. About another 10 percent was honest and incorruptible no matter what. The remaining 80 percent wished they were honest.

While attending a training school in 1966, Durk met plainclothes officer Frank Serpico. That chance meeting would eventually result in this country's most publicized investigation into systemic police bribery and corruption that took place in the New York city police department in the 1960s and early 1970s. Durk and Serpico exposed the practice of police officers using their positions to extract money and gifts from gamblers and mobsters. The story was popularized in the 1973 Hollywood film, "*Serpico*," starring Al Pacino.

New York Police Detective Third Grade Frank Serpico was particularly unique, according to his biographer Peter Maas. "He was the first officer in the history of the Police Department who not only reported corruption in its ranks, but actually stepped forward to testify about it in court."

Durk's biographer, James Lardner, in his book *Crusader*, made clear that Durk knew about the history of corruption in the police department. He was aware, for example, that back in the 1890s, according to the Lexow Committee, the police were involved in selling protection to gamblers and others and even in extorting payoffs from these people. More than half a century later (and three big police-corruption scandals) later, the situation was essentially unchanged. There existed what was called a "code of silence" among the police where cops "on the pad" (taking money) were simply not talked about by other cops (Lardner, 1996).

In 1969, Durk was one of sixteen detectives and superior officers on special assignment to New York City's Department of Investigation, an agency which was independent of the police department. In this capacity he was able to gain a particularly accurate but sad view of many of the corrupt undertakings of police detectives operating in narcotics, most notably in East Harlem, and specifically on Pleasant Avenue.

In his book *The Pleasant Avenue Connection*, Durk related how, during the 1960s, "Pleasant Avenue was a street that never closed down. If you knew the right people, you could go there at three in the morning and borrow fifty thousand dollars in cash or rent a sub-machine gun or arrange to fix a judge or pick up three kilos of heroin" (Durk, 1976, p. 27).

According to Durk, many police officers and detectives were intimately tied up in the drug trade. "If a middle-level drug dealer wanted to buy a kilo of heroin in New York, he could buy it from a Mafia dealer on Pleasant Avenue – or from a cop assigned to the Special Investigations Unit [at the First Precinct station house]," Durk discovered (Durk, 1976, p. 28).

Starting on April 25, 1970, and for weeks afterwards, the police corruption story made New York front page news and necessitated action by Mayor John Lindsay as well as by the NYPD. The scandal shook the city. The newspapers told of gambling bosses, pimps, drug dealers and business people systematically paying officers and supervisors for protection or favors, and of the police and City Hall officials failing to act on evidence.

New York was by no means unique in its experience of systemic corruption. Around the time this scandal was breaking, 30 police officers in New Orleans were charged with bribery and conspiracy to protect organized gambling and vice; in Seattle, 100 officers, including the assistant chief of police, were involved in a shakedown system; and Boston, Washington D.C., Chicago, Atlanta, Baltimore, San Francisco, Philadelphia, Newark, and Louisville all experienced police department corruption scandals.

Indeed, almost every serious history of policing has had to deal with the existence of police graft and corruption. Corruption has been more visible at certain times in history than others. It has also been more lethal and deep-rooted in certain jurisdictions than others.

There are a number of factors which make police officers particularly vulnerable to corruption. The first of these is that police officers are continuously brought into contact with lawbreakers who have a vested interest in how well the police perform their enforcement and investigatory functions. Another reason is that police officers possess a considerable amount of discretionary authority that is not always adequately supervised. Due to the dangerous and sometimes confusing situations which a police officer must face, the need for quick judgment calls is essential. Such on-the-spot decisions are frequently a matter of "art" for the officer and not a result of written rules or procedures.

The number of different duties which a police officer may be called on to perform is almost endless. He is continually placed in situations where he must make life-or-death decisions involving frightened, angry, confused, injured, violent, and mentally ill people. When an officer takes command and control of a situation, he must often decide who is telling the truth, who started the problem, who must be cited, and who must be arrested. Because of this, they are presented with numerous opportunities where the pressure and temptation to act corruptly are thrust upon them.

But seeing corruption and actually doing something about it are two totally different things. There are powerful organizational factors which make it very difficult for a police officer to "rat out" other officers. One of the most inherent and pervasive tenets of the police culture is loyalty. This "blue wall of silence" reinforces the need of every officer to heed the unwritten code of silence.

Whistleblowing is not an easy thing to do. There are almost always dire consequences to whistleblowers, to their careers, and to their personal lives as a result of their actions. Many organizations make whistleblowing a very difficult thing to do, and a police department is one of these organizations.

Durk and Serpico broke the blue wall of silence. Their five-year battle with corruption in the New York Police Department ended with the Knapp Commission hearings in 1970 which exposed the deeply ingrained culture of graft and official indifference that existed in the department.

"At the very beginning, the most important fact to understand," testified Durk before the Knapp Commission, "is that I had and have no special knowledge of police corruption . . . The facts were there waiting to be exposed. This commission, to its enormous credit, has exposed them.

". . . The fact is that almost wherever we turned in the police department, wherever we turned in the city administration, and almost wherever we went in the rest of the city, we were met not with cooperation, not with appreciation, not with eagerness to seek out the truth, but with suspicion and hostility and laziness and inattention . . ." The average cop, he testified, longed to be honest but felt that "he lives in the middle of a corrupt society." He expressed that the department was one in which "men who could have been good officers, men of decent impulse . . . were told in a hundred ways every day, 'Go along, forget about the law, don't make waves and shut up . . .'" (Durk, 1976, p. 27).

"To the sordid record of police corruption unveiled by the Knapp Commission has now been added an even more depressing saga of official indifference born of the apparent belief that graft was so ingrained it was better left unchallenged," *The New York Times* editorialized.

The indifference regarding police corruption in the New York police Department, according to David Durk, went all the way up to the mayor's office. Indeed, many say that it was the Knapp Commission together with the testimony of Durk and Serpico, that prematurely ended Mayor Lindsay's hopes for a presidential bid in 1972.

Durk was always, and continues to be, tremendously committed to the inherent altruism in police work and to the desire to do good. "Being a cop . . . means serving, helping others," he testified to the Knapp Commission. ". . . to be a cop is to help an old lady walk the street safely, to help a twelve-year-old girl reach her next birthday without being gang-raped, to help the storekeeper make a living without keeping a shotgun under his cash register, to help a boy grow up without needles in his arm."

"Once, I arrested a landlord's agent," Durk told the Knapp Commission, "who offered to pay me if I would lock up a tenant who was organizing other tenants in the building. As I put the cuffs on the agent and led him away, a crowd of people gathered around and actually shouted, "Viva la policia!" This is what it means to be a policeman.

Elson Gelfand

Elson Gelfand entered the New York City Police Academy in 1959 as one of five Jews of a class of 500 men. "There were so few Jews that it was pathetic," says Gelfand questioning why, in a city like New York where there are so many Jews, there should be so few Jews on the police department. He thinks the reason for this is that "Jewish parents had higher goals in mind for their sons" than becoming cops. For Gelfand, growing up in the Fort Greene section of New York City, becoming a cop was about the only way he could stop all the gentile kids from picking on him. But this did not make it any easier on his family who wanted him to go into his father-in-law's business.

Gelfand's first assignment as a patrolman was the 28th precinct in upper Manhattan. But "upper Manhattan" meant Harlem. "I was a Jewish kid, what did I know from Harlem?" he thought at the time. But he tried the best he could and actually did quite well. He also returned to college, graduating from Brooklyn College with a bachelor's degree in education in 1962 and a masters in education in 1965. In 1969 Gelfand was promoted to sergeant and assigned to the 110th precinct in the Bronx (also called Fort Apache). Given his teacher education, he was

also assigned to teach at the police academy. One of the special projects he was involved in was assisting returning Vietnam-era vets obtain
their GEDs and enter the police department (E. Gelfand, personal communication, January 10, 2006).

Gelfand was promoted to lieutenant and went to Internal Affairs in
1973. This was just around the time of the Knapp Commission and all
the associated investigations. Although he had no first hand knowledge
of police payoffs or corruption, he had heard stories. Most of these had
to do with cops at the precinct level who accepted money from businessmen who needed breaks for parking and making deliveries. It usually
consisted of "a couple of bucks here and there" but not the major money
exposed by the Knapp Commission in gambling and narcotics. He could
not understand these cops who would jeopardize their careers and their
pensions by accepted money, and referred to them as "grass eaters" (E.
Gelfand, personal communication, January 10, 2006).

The term "grass eater" often appears in the law enforcement and
criminal justice literature describing one of the various levels of police
corruption. In their book *Police Corruption and Psychological Testing*,
Natalie L. Claussen-Rogers and Bruce Arrigo definitively define
these various levels of corruption.

Officers showing the least severe level of corruption are referred to
as White Knights. Such officers are supposedly honest to a fault.
However, they often hold extreme ethical opinions and are rigid and
judgmental. Such a high degree or rigidity often results in morale
problems in the police organization.

The Straight Shooter is next in the continuum of severity. These are
"honest" cops who are inclined to overlook the indiscretions of other
officers. The usually do not want to create problems for the police department and they feel a sense of loyalty toward their fellow officers.

The next group is called Grass Eaters. These officers engage in some
corrupt activities as the opportunity arises and accept payoffs available to officers. They primarily engage in accepting gratuities,
occasional kickbacks, and opportunistic thefts. They often tend to be

the heart of the corruption problem due to the great numbers who engage in these activities.

Meat Eaters actively seek out opportunities for corruption. They aggressively misuse their authority for personal gain and tend to seek out activities which will produce money and personal benefits. They come to work with the idea of making illegal money. They enjoy the experience of unlimited authority that stems from feeling immune to the law or any rules.

The final group of corrupt officers is called Rogue Officers. This group is thoroughly corrupt and operates without any ethics or morals. They often commit highly visible shakedowns of citizens, felony fixes, and direct criminal activities (p.25).

Gelfand was friends with David Durk. He recalls receiving phone calls from Durk regarding his exposing police corruption and testifying against other cops, "I'm doing the right thing, aren't I?" He would ask over and over again. This is something Durk took very seriously and was constantly worried about. He knew that he and Serpico were making history by blowing the lid off what was going on in the department. He also knew that he was doing one of the worst things a cop can ever do – testify against other cops.

In 1981 Gelfand was promoted to captain. This is the highest civil service rank in the New York City police department. After this all promotions were appointments and supposedly based on experience and merit but in reality were based on "who you know and who likes you." One person that liked Gelfand was the Brooklyn District Attorney Eugene Gold. Gelfand describes Gold as being a "tough Jew" who ran a tight ship and wanted things done right and by the book all the way down the line (E. Gelfand, personal communication, January 10, 2006).

Gold personally requested Gelfand to be the commanding officer of the DA's office for two reasons. The first was because of his excellent reputation for honesty and hard work established while in Internal Affairs. The second reason (told to him by Gold himself) was that he wanted a Jewish boss in the District Attorney's office.

Gelfand was transferred to the 13th Precinct (Grammercy Park) in 1984 as the commanding officer. In 1985 he was appointed a Deputy Inspector and went to the 6th Precinct in Manhattan South. In 1987 he was appointed a full Inspector and sent to an administrative position in Queens. In 1988 he was requested by then Police Commissioner Benjamin Ward to take control of the 9th Precinct which contained Tompkins Square Park. The park had been the scene of the infamous Tompkins Square riots.

Tompkins Square Park is a 10.5 acre public park in the Alphabet City section of the East Village in Manhattan. It is bounded on the north by East 10th Street, on the east by Avenue B, on the south by East 7th Street, and on the west by Avenue A. The park has long been a center for political activism and was the site of demonstrations against the Vietnam War in the 1960s. It is also the place where Indian Sadhu A.C. Bhaktivedanta Swami Prabhupada came to sing and preach in 1965, which began the worldwide Hare Krishna movement.

In the 1980s Tompkins Square Park had become for many New Yorkers synonymous with the city's increased social problems. The park at that time was a high-crime area that contained encampments of homeless people, and it was a center for illegal drug dealing and heroin use.

In August 1988, riots erupted when police attempted to clear the park of homeless people. Forty-four people were injured during the melees. On August 6 and August 7 numerous bystanders, homeless people and political activists protested.

There were charges of police brutality when a large number of police surrounded the park and charged at the hemmed-in crowd while other police ordered all pedestrians not to walk on streets neighboring the park. Hundreds of activists as well as innocent bystanders joined together in chants of "No police state" and "It's our park, you don't live here!" Much of the violence was videotaped and clips were shown on local TV news reports (notably including one by a man who sat on his stoop across the street from the park and continued to film while a police officer beat him up), but ultimately, although at least one case went to trial, no police officers were convicted.

The Tompkins Square melee revealed political, economic, and cultural tensions among class- and ethnic-based resident factions over ways to deal with or combat real estate intentions and actions, and the city's local development policies. Gelfand was part of the cleaning-up process, which helped to restore order to the area. Then mayor Ed Koch gave orders to clean up the park and would often personally visit to evaluate the progress. At times Gelfand would be out in the area and "I would look up and there he was with his entourage," said Gelfand referring to Koch (E. Gelfand, personal communication, January 10, 2006).

Over the next ten years, with increased gentrification in the East Village, as well as enforcement of a park curfew, the eviction of homeless people, and refurbishment, the character of Tompkins Square Park changed considerably for the better. But while the memory of the riots was still fresh in the minds of most New Yorkers, the Crown Heights section of Brooklyn would erupt with tragic and deadly results.

What is now Crown Heights used to be called Crow Hill (when newly freed slaves settled there prior to the civil war). The area had traditionally been populated by Irish, Italians, and Jewish-Americans who began a wholesale exodus in the 1960s and 1970s. Upon their departure for the suburbs, Crown Heights became home to three main groups of people. One of the groups were African-Americans coming up from the South, most notably from North and South Carolina. Another group was immigrants from the Caribbean. The third group was the sect of Hassidic Jews known as the Lubavitchers.

Most Hassidic Jews arrived in America in the 1880s as part of the great Jewish emigration that brought 2.5 million Eastern European Jews to America between 1880 and 1925. Many of these ultra-orthodox Hassidic Jews also came here around the time of World War II to escape the Nazi onslaught.

In 1940, Rabbi Yosef Yitzchak Schneersohn, the sixth Lubavitcher Rebbe, entered New York to set up the court of Chabad-Lubavitch in America. After the Rebbe's arrival, America's Lubavitcher population soared. In Crown Heights, by the late 1960s, the Lubavitchers were the only Jews that remained.

Following the death of the sixth Lubavitcher Rebbe, the spiritual leader of the Lubavitchers became Rebbe Menachem Schneerson, who asked his followers to remain in the Crown Heights neighborhood (He himself never left Brooklyn). By 1991, the only whites remaining in Crown Heights were the fifteen thousand members of this sect. They constituted about ten percent of the neighborhood population.

In 1991, Gelfand was a one-star Chief and executive officer in Brooklyn South which included Crown Heights. It was on his watch that the tumultuous events of August 19th, 1991 ensued.

On that evening, a car in the entourage of the Chabad Rebbe Menachem Mendel Schneerson, led by an unmarked police car, either ran a red light or passed through a yellow one. Rabbi Schneerson was returning from a visit to his father-in-law's grave (his predecessor), when one of the cars was hit by another car, causing it to veer out of control and strike Gavin Cato, a seven-year old Guyanese boy who subsequently died of his injuries.

A private Hassidic ambulance came to the scene and removed the Hassidic driver on the orders of a police officer, who, while attempting to lift the car off the child, was assaulted by angry bystanders. A city ambulance arrived minutes later to treat Gavin, who died of his injuries a few hours later.

What ensued was a three-day, four-night anti-Semitic riot also known as the "Crown Heights pogrom" by members of the Jewish community. Fires were set and shops were looted as the riot grew out of control and as the mob's rage continued.

Published accounts reveal that on one night, on Carroll Street between Brooklyn and Kingston Avenues, a young Jewish man was surrounded by fifteen blacks, who kicked him and struck him with bottles and rocks while chanting "Jews get out of here." On President Street, returning home with her three small children, a Jewish woman was cornered by black youths chanting "Heil Hitler!" and "Kill the Jews!" (Wikipedia, Crown Heights, p.1)

During the riots, at least 188 Hassidic Jews were attacked and many were seriously injured by rioting African-American residents of the neighborhood, presumably because of unequal treatment of the car wreck victims. Included among the victims was a visiting rabbinical student from Australia by the name of Yankel Rosenbaum, 29 years old, who had come to continue study on the Holocaust.

Before dying, Rosenbaum was able to identify 16-year-old Lemrick Nelson, Jr. as his assailant. Nelson was charged with the killing, but later acquitted in state court. Apparently, claims that he admitted to having stabbed Rosenbaum were dismissed by the jury. After protests by the Lubavitch community and others, Nelson was charged in federal court with violating Rosenbaum's civil rights and received a prison sentence of 19.5 years. In 2002, he was granted a new trial, at which he admitted he stabbed Rosenbaum, but his attorneys argued that the stabbing wasn't a hate crime triggered by Rosenbaum's religion, but rather the consequence of Nelson being intoxicated at the time.

Another man, Charles Price, 44, was charged with inciting the mob, including Nelson, to "get Jews". Price was charged in federal court one day before the expiration of the statute of limitations. He was released to a halfway house on June 5, 2004.

In addition to the Rosenbaum murder, during the rioting, a 67-year-old non-Jewish motorist who had apparently gotten lost in the neighborhood, Anthony Graziosi, had been dragged out of his car and brutally beaten and stabbed to death, presumably because his full beard and dark clothing had caused his killers to mistake him for a Hassidic Jew. No suspects have ever been apprehended in his murder.

Then mayor David Dinkins, and along with him the Police Department, were criticized for the poor handling of the events in Crown Heights. The turmoil proved to be a key issue in the next New York City mayoral election in which Dinkins was defeated by Rudolph Giuliani, whom Dinkins had narrowly defeated four years earlier.

Eventually, especially following the election of Giuliani, tempers and attitudes relating to the Crown Heights affair cooled down. Accomplished performance artist and actress Anna Deavere Smith wrote a one-woman play, "Fires in the Mirror", about the racial tensions in Crown Heights after the riots. In a series of brief monologues, Ms.

Smith presented 29 characters based on verbatim excerpts from interviews conducted with her subjects. The play facilitated an intercultural exchange and public discussion about sexual and racial politics, ethnic identity, and multiculturalism.

Chief Gelfand had a good relationship with the Chabad Rabbe Schneerson and knew him personally. In 1992, Schneerson invited him to Chabad headquarters at 770 Eastern Parkway for a talk. "[He] took my hand and thanked me," said Gelfand. "He had a tremendous presence about him and was a fine man."

Gelfand would at times stop by "770" just to show a presence. He recalls one such visit fondly. "There I was in full uniform, a star on each shoulder and all that fancy stuff on my hat, and the first thing they said to me was 'Did you put on tefillin today' and 'Come let's daven.'"

Gelfand retired from the police department in 1997 at age 63 as a one star chief. Now 72, he lives on Long Island and spends a good deal of time volunteering as a special education teacher in Nassau County. Every Tuesday he also volunteers at the Bronx zoo with "a bunch of other alter cockers" (E. Gelfand, personal communication, January 10, 2006).

Howard Safir

In 1994 Howard Safir was asked by Mayor Rudolph Giuliani to serve as New York City's 29th Fire Commissioner. Then in 1996, following the resignation of Bill Bratton, he was appointed as the 39th Police Commissioner of New York City.

Safir grew up in the Bronx and Long Island. As was the case with many Jews of his era, his grandparents were religious (from Russia) but his parents were more like cultural Jews. But Safir did have a Bar Mitzvah and attended Hebrew school.

Despite the fact that his uncle Lou Weiser was a Detective with the NYPD, going into law enforcement was not his family's wishes for young Safir, in fact, his mother "took to bed" upon learning the news of his wanting to be a federal agent. He began his law enforcement career in 1965 as a special agent assigned to the New York office of the Federal Bureau of Narcotics, a forerunner of the Drug Enforcement Administration (DEA) (H. Safir, personal communication, March 10, 2004).

Safir was somewhat of an idealist, thinking, even at the young age of 23, that he could have a serious impact on the world's crime problems. While with the Bureau of Narcotics, he worked a series of daring undercover stints, including one as a hippie drug buyer in San Francisco's Haight-Ashbury district. He advanced through the ranks of the DEA and in 1977 was appointed assistant director. While with the DEA Safir never detected any pressure to keep a low profile because of being Jewish. "Everybody was identified by their religion, it was an open thing" he recalled (H. Safir, personal communication, March 10, 2004).

After the DEA Safir moved to the U.S. Marshal's Service where he worked some famous cases and brought many notorious individuals to justice. These included Christopher Boyce (the "Falcon" of the Falcon and the Snowman), and ex-C.I.A. agent turned Libyan stooge Edwin Wilson. He eventually became associate director for operations, supervising everything from courthouse security to fugitive retrieval. He later served as chief of the Witness Security Division of the U.S. Marshals Service and was responsible for making vital changes to the program which are still in effect to this day. He retired from the federal government in 1990.

In his four years as New York police commissioner, Safir achieved a 38% reduction in major crime and a 44% reduction in homicides. But 1999 brought trouble for Safir and his boss Giuliani when Jewish police detective Eric Turetzky blew the cover off of one of the biggest stories in the New York City police department of the last twenty-five years – the Abner Louima case.

In revealing what he saw and knew in the Louima police brutality case, and by testifying against other cops, Eric Turetzky did the one unthinkable thing only a few others have braved to do—he broke the infamous "blue wall of silence" that exists among police officers. The events of that hot summer night in 1997 are truly a blot on the history of the NYPD.

Haitian immigrant Abner Louima had gone out to a popular dance club called Club Rendezvous, in the Flatbush section of Brooklyn. As the band stopped playing, a fight broke out and the police soon arrived. Among the many officers who showed up was Eric Turetzky, who was then a rookie police officer.

During the struggle one officer was knocked down by a punch. Meanwhile Abner Louima, who was supposedly speaking out against the police knocking another man down, was beaten, arrested, cuffed, and placed into a radio car by several of the officers. As Louima was driven to the 70th precinct he was allegedly taunted by officers with racial epithets and told to go back to Haiti. They mistakenly reported over their radio that they had the person who had knocked down the officer in custody. Louima would later testify that that the two police officers transporting him to the precinct house had allegedly stopped the car twice in order to beat him with their fists and portable radios.

At 4:35 in the morning, Louima was brought into the precinct house. From this point forward, many police officers and civilian employees were present and were likely aware of the events that were about to transpire. At the front desk of the precinct house, several officers supposedly removed Louima's belt and pulled his pants and underwear down to his ankles. The desk sergeant later testified that the officer who processed Louima then led him away.

Detective Turetzky later testified that he saw Louima being taken from the front desk to the back of the precinct, then down a small hallway where the only unlocked room was the bathroom. One of the officers present would testify that he was asked for a pair of leather gloves by one of the two officers before Louima was led to the bathroom and that the gloves were later returned covered with blood. Civilian precinct employees gave similar accounts in their testimonies.

Abner Louima would later testify that once in the bathroom he was allegedly severely assaulted by two officers. He claimed that the assault consisted of being kicked in the groin and brutally and savagely sodomized with a toilet plunger stick.

Bleeding heavily, his insides torn, Louima was thrown into a cell. He was allegedly told by one of the officers that if he told anybody about what was done to him, both he and his family would be hunted down and killed. But Louima did tell, in whispered Haitian Creole, to a Haitian nurse at a hospital where he was taken following the assault. It was this nurse who originally notified the Internal Affairs unit of the police department. No other witnesses were willing to come forward at that point.

"He said what he saw, and that's what a cop is supposed to do," said Sergeant Eric Finkelstein, president of the New York Shomrim Society, of Eric Turetzky. In the same *New York Times* article it was reported that Jewish police officers were standing firmly behind one of their own who breached the blue wall of silence in the Louima case. . . " (March 8, 2000).

Finkelstein said he was unaware of any concern about a backlash against Jewish cops following Turetzky's trial testimony. "If these guys did what they are accused of doing, I can't imagine any cop that's going to defend them," said Finkelstein, who worked in the operations division at police headquarters (March 8, 2000).

Prior to the Louima trial and Turetzky's testimony, Jewish officers and the Shomrim Society had complained to then Police Commissioner Howard Safir of growing anti-Semitism in the police department which had not been addressed. In this context, Turetzky's coming forward to provide crucial testimony in the racially explosive Louima case made some Jewish cops uneasy. But Finkelstein said he was aware of no one in Shomrim who felt that Turetzky should not have come forward.

When a second officer testified for the prosecution, Turetzky was taken somewhat out of the spotlight. "If they were going to say, 'Look, only Jews turn people in,' another guy testifying will make that [more difficult]," said Finkelstein. "People who see it that way would have seen it that way anyway. I don't think it's going to be a big problem, if it becomes a problem at all."

Rabbi Alvin Kass, the NYPD's Jewish chaplain and spiritual adviser to Shomrim, who had a close relationship with Turetzky, described him as a "very warm, caring person and an extremely courageous young man." "I got to know him well as a result of this, and he can serve as a role model for today's generation" (March 8, 2000).

Rabbi Kass said other Jewish cops he'd spoken with welcomed and embraced Turetzky's actions. He cited another cop with the same last name as saying "I'm not related to him, but I would be proud if I was."

Kass, who instructs academy recruits in police ethics, predicted that these events would make cops like Turetzky more the rule than the exception, as the notorious blue wall of silence crumbles.

"We're on the threshold of an era in which it's understood that honesty and integrity and truth are indispensable for effective law enforcement," said Rabbi Kass (March 8, 2000).

Another major problem for Commissioner Safir took place in 1999. In that year, four members of the citywide Street Crime Unit decided to investigate what they construed as the suspicious behavior of twenty-two-year-old Amadou Diallo, who was standing near the entrance of an apartment building in the Soundview section of the Bronx. As the plainclothes officers approached, Diallo reached into his pocket and removed an object which appeared to at least one of the officers to be a gun. The object turned out to be a wallet but it was too late for Diallo as the officers unloaded 41 rounds in his direction killing him instantly.

The officers involved in the Diallo shooting were tried on charges of second-degree murder. Due to the angry spirit in the community, the venue for the trial had to be changed to Albany where a jury of eight whites and four blacks acquitted all four officers on all charges in February, 2000.

Within a few weeks of the verdict, two more unarmed African-American men were killed by undercover narcotics officers, setting off yet another round of harsh community protests. This incident, together with the entire Diallo affair revealed a major divide between the police and the black and Hispanic residents of New York.

Most police officers saw the Diallo incident as a terrible accident that could happen to any police officer at any time. There was no malice or racial element present at all for most cops. But many blacks, Hispanics, and some whites expressed that this was one more example of how all it took was being a young black male in order to draw the attention (and the fire) of white police officers.

Safir did order changes in the Street Crime Unit following the Diallo killing. For a while officers in the unit were even put back in uniform. But he defended the unit's mission, usefulness, and effectiveness in helping to rid the city of guns on the street. Eventually the police department was able to get back to the business of dealing effectively with the community – white, black, and Hispanic alike.

Howard Safir is presently chairman and chief executive officer of SafirRosetti, Omnicom Group, Inc., a security and investigation company. Safir is also consultant to the chair of ChoicePoint, a provider of credential verification and identification services.

Safir is proud of the fact that he was the first (and only) Jewish police commissioner with the NYPD. "So many cops were Italian but the Jews were the ones that scored high on the exams" and got promoted. Although, he adds, "sometimes they had to sue the department to get it."

He identifies with being a Jew but is not religious and does not belong to a temple. His wife is Catholic. Yet he sees the cultural aspects and traditions of his Jewish background as being responsible to some degree for his success. These include strong family ties, compassion for others, a need to excel and be better than his peers, and "lots of guilt" (H. Safir, personal communication, March 10, 2004).

Joanne Jaffe

On August 1, 2003, Joanne Jaffe became the first woman (Jew or non-Jew) three-star chief in the New York City Police Department.

Jaffe was born in the Bayside area of Queens in New York into a Jewish family. Her neighborhood, like so many other Queens neighborhoods, was Jewish and Italian. Although her family was not particularly religious, they went to services on the holidays and made sure that she knew about her Jewish heritage. She most certainly know about how her grandparents came to this country from Russia and Poland and what they went through in the process.

Jaffe attended the John Jay College of Criminal Justice and graduated in 1979. That same year she entered the New York City police department as a recruit. Her family was not exactly thrilled with her decision to pursue police work, they had wanted her to be a teacher (she has a sister who is a doctor and a brother who is a lawyer). In the police academy Jaffe was one of 20 women out of 445 recruits. Her first assignment was a foot patrol beat in the neighborhood stabilization unit, an assignment she loved. What really made this assignment exciting and challenging was the constant community interaction and chance to see things up close and have a direct impact on people's lives.

In those early days female officers were just coming into their own and were not completely accepted by many factions within the police department. Jaffe sees fighting to get what she wants as being a continual theme of her police career. For example, in 1980 she fought to be assigned a radio car along with another female officer, something that was relatively unheard of at that time. After much resistance she was eventually given permission for this. But while on patrol together something "terrible" happened to them – not a homicide or a shooting, but worse – they had a flat tire. She can't remember how many male cops drove by and laughed at the two apparently helpless female cops waiting by the side of the road in a radio car for someone to rescue them. But they didn't need any rescuing, they changed their own flat and continued with their tour (J. Jaffe, personal communication, April 10, 2004).

Actually, on the two women's first day on patrol together they successfully responded to an armed robbery call. After making the arrest, they walked the handcuffed gunman into the precinct past the disbelieving stares of their colleagues who had initially resisted and criticized their assignment. This was a pivotal moment in Jaffe's career because it proved to others and herself that she could do the job.

One of Jaffe's favorite assignments was in the 75th Precinct in the East New York section of Brooklyn. She recalls that she "loved it from the beginning" because it involved everything she wanted to do as a police officer. She was constantly busy, on the go, and locking up bad guys. At the same she was concentrating on the part of police work she feels is the most important – being a social worker or a psychologist – being the first line of assistance for people who needed help in any and all kinds of situations.

After serving in the Organized Crime Bureau in narcotics, Jaffe was promoted to sergeant in 1985 and assigned to the 104th precinct in Queens. Sergeants in precinct houses are not involved in the daily nuts and bolts of police work on the streets and they don't make arrests. Therefore, this was not her favorite assignment. But in 1988 she was assigned to the Street Crimes Unit which she describes as "heaven" because it allowed her to work all over the city but most of all, she was back in the middle of things on the street (J. Jaffe, personal communication, April 10, 2004).

In 1989 Jaffe was promoted to lieutenant and assigned to the 115th Precinct in Jackson Heights. She attended the FBI National Academy in 1989 and was promoted to Captain soon after. After excelling in various other assignments, she was promoted to her present position as Chief of the Housing Bureau in 2003. Commissioner Ray Kelly said "Chief Jaffe is an outstanding leader who has excelled in a series of commands, . . . I am confident that she will continue to raise the standards of excellence and professionalism in her new capacity."

Chief Jaffe still loves coming to work every day. She is very proud of her accomplishments and feels that she has worked hard to achieve them. Looking back, she can laugh now at how she was considered the black sheep of her family for being a Jewish woman cop. She recalls that her grandmother was "mortified" by her decision and would not tell anyone that her granddaughter was a cop, she would just say "this is my granddaughter Joanne, she has a master's degree." However, her family's pride only increased with each of her promotions (J. Jaffe, personal communication, October 10, 2005).

Although serving in a high-level command position is important to her, Jaffe particularly enjoys being a role model for other officers and assisting them in any way that she can. It is interesting that after the last 26 years, with all the different jobs and all the promotions, she still considers herself a "street cop" which is probably her proudest job after all.

Robert Morgenthau

When Robert Morgenthau graduated from law school, he became an assistant to Robert Patterson, former secretary of the army, at Patterson's law firm. As Patterson and Morgenthau were heading for LaGuardia Airport on a business trip, Patterson saw that he had left important documents at the office. He asked Morgenthau to return to the office for them and take a later flight. Patterson died that afternoon when his plane crashed. The rest is, as they say, history.

Robert Morgenthau has carried the badge of the chief law enforcement officer of New York County for nearly thirty years. His badge is unblemished, as he has received nothing but praise and respect from all those who work for him and around him. And at age 87 there is no sign that he will be quitting any time soon.

Robert Morris Morgenthau was born in New York City on July 31, 1919 into a highly regarded family in both the political arena as well as in the Jewish community. His father, Henry Morgenthau, would later serve under Presidents Roosevelt and Truman as the Secretary of the Treasury. His grandfather had been the U.S. ambassador to Turkey. Morgenthau grew up cooking hot dogs with Eleanor Roosevelt and mixing mint juleps for Winston Churchill. Despite his political exposure, he never felt any pressure from his family to enter the political arena or the law.

By the time Morgenthau went to college in 1937, the events of the Holocaust became the focus of his attention, and he wanted to get involved in the effort to destroy the Nazi war machine. In the spring of his junior year at Amherst College, he signed on with the U.S. Navy but had to get his parents' approval because he was under 21. He spent his 21st birthday aboard the battleship USS Wyoming in Guantanamo Bay, Cuba.

Morgenthau would spend the next four years on destroyers meeting people from all over the country and acquiring great responsibility very quickly. After being on active duty for only a year and half, by the summer of 1943 he became Executive Officer and Navigator of a destroyer supervising 299 men. He also became the court martial officer aboard ship and learned about the art of plea bargaining. Morgenthau practiced Judaism openly and with pride in the military and never encountered much religious animosity and he was always intolerant of any form of racial or ethnic biases around him.

After the war, Morgenthau left the Navy with the rank of Lieutenant Commander and enrolled in Yale Law School, from where he would later graduate with much distinction. He would spend the next 13 years learning his trade at the firm of Patterson, Belknap & Webb.

Morgenthau left the private sector on April 19, 1961 when his boyhood friend President John F. Kennedy appointed him United States Attorney for the Southern District of New York. This position yielded power and respect and allowed him to gain the trust of the people of New York City. With only a brief break to run for governor, he stayed in the high-profile prosecutor's job through 1970. He was elected New York County's District Attorney in January of 1975 and has served in this capacity all these years up to and including the present.

The District Attorney's office investigates and prosecutes a myriad of crimes which occur in New York County. Some of the types of crimes confronting the office depends on what is generally happening in the streets. In 1985 this included most notably narcotics and street gangs.

In their book *NYPD, A City and its Police*, James Lardiner and Thomas Reppetto discussed in depth the appearance on the streets of New York a group of young men calling themselves the "Vigilantes" who began robbing and killing drug dealers in upper Manhattan in the mid 1980s. The group's announced mission was to "get rid of the drug dealers" but their actual intent was to install their own people in their place. By 1985, the Vigilantes numbered thirty members and about twenty four associate members.

The group began wearing green military-like uniforms with black Army "jump boots." They even had their own rank insignia – a silver hatchet on a chain around the neck for soldiers, a gold one for lieutenants and above.

Margenthau's office set up a special homicide investigation unit after the murder of a witness who was about to testify for the state at the murder trial of one of the gang members. The DA eventually successfully prosecuted a number of Vigilantes and obtained sentences of twenty-five years to life.

The special homicide investigation unit also went after some of the infamous drug syndicate operations which were running rampant in New York City in the 1990s. Forty percent of the annual two thousand murders in the city were drug-related. Most of these crimes were handled by the police department's homicide or narcotics squad. But these squads did not have much of an impact on the young drug syndicates that kept popping up all over the place. Much of the work busting these groups was done by Morgenthau's office.

One of the individuals on the DA's hit list was a murderous gunman known on the streets as "Freddy Krueger" who had allegedly murdered at least seven people in 1992 alone. He apparently eluded police custody several times and in 1993 was caught near the George Washington Bridge carrying a nine-millimeter weapon. He was arrested and released pending trial. He disappeared soon thereafter and was later captured in the Dominican Republic, after committing a murder there.

Morgenthau has always been involved with community and Jewish philanthropic causes including the Police Athletic League, Temple Emanuel-El, the Federation of Jewish Philanthropies, the ADL, and the Museum of Jewish Heritage. He was also asked by Mayor Ed Koch to be co-chairman of a commission charged with planning how New York could memorialize those who had perished in the Holocaust. Morgenthau has been known to say that if you want people to understand Israel, they had to first understand the Holocaust.

Morgenthau's tremendous contributions to justice, and his impact on New York City has been acknowledged in the television show *Law and Order* where the role of the District Attorney as played by Adam Schiff was based on him. As the Manhattan DA Morgenthau oversees more than 550 assistant district attorneys, along with a support staff of another 700, and the office prosecutes more than 130,000 criminal cases annually.

Mr. Morgenthau's major problem in 2005 was his election battle against 63-year old judge Leslie Crocker Snyder, who waged an aggressive campaign to unseat him. Part of Morgenthau's platform was that he had not yet accomplished the mission he began in 1975 when he was first elected District Attorney when Abe Beam was the mayor of New York City. The voters agreed and he won reelection 59 to 41 percent.

Morgenthau, or "the boss" to anyone who works with him, heads up one of the most experienced investigative teams in the country. The people that work for him are also loyal, and this stability has allowed for more thorough, long-term investigations in all areas of criminal activity including money laundering, terrorism, and identity theft.

In an interview with the *New York Observer*, Mr. Morgenthau discussed his philosophy when it comes to terrorism. He believes that by stopping money laundering, terrorists are being suffocated for the funds they need to carry out their attacks. He feels that much of these crimes fall under his jurisdiction since much of this money passes through New York banks. "Courts can decide if we have jurisdiction or not," he said, responding to criticism that he is overstepping his bounds. "It is not for us to abdicate responsibility where we have it."

No matter what disagreements some people may have with Morgenthau or his tactics, "he is universally recognized as the nation's top prosecutor," says ex-mayor Ed Koch. "One thing, above all, that you know with Bob Morgenthau: he has only one client, the public" (Jewish Virtual Library, 2005).

Jane Perlov

Of the 1,000 members of the 1981 New York City police academy class, about 40 were women and considerably less were Jews, Jane Perlov was both. In a way only a Jewish mother could, Perlov's mother told her to "take good notes" because one day she will want to write a book. Her mother knew of course, that this job was only temporary until her middle daughter became an accomplished lawyer or author (J. Perlov, personal communication, December 13, 2005).

Perlov grew up in Queens and Manhattan in a non-religious but very "Jewish" home. She wasn't exactly sure what she wanted to do with her life but did know that she had to graduate college and do something which helped people. "Helping people was a tradition in our family" she recalls as her parents provided examples in their own lives of service and honor. Unlike many of the Irish cops that she would later work with, Perlov could not just point to a family tradition of police work as her motivation for the job.

In 1991, as a Captain, Perlov reported for work at the Midtown South precinct of Times Square. When she first walked into the office of her new boss, Inspector Michael Fox, she thought she was a goner. There he was, sitting there with his feet up on the desk, a cigar stuffed in his mouth, and with big white eyebrows that seemed to go in all directions. She could only imagine what he would think about "this young chick" (J. Perlov, personal communication, December 13, 2005).

Michael Fox turned out to be one of Perlov's most understanding and memorable mentors on the police department. Under his command she was to become instrumental in saving Times Square and making it the safe and cleaner place that it remains to this day. This took a lot of work but she was out there every night. She was the only uniformed police Captain in the entire city who actually patrolled the streets. But for anyone who knows her this is no surprise as she has always been a hands-on person who deals with situations and people face-to-face. In fact, she has always, and still does, consider herself a "street cop."

Perlov's other mentor on the police department was Bill Bratton who was the Police Commissioner in 1994. What she particularly admired about him was the way he challenged the people under him. This was especially true for women to whom he would always give difficult assignments and push to their limits. This was just fine with Perlov as she was attracted to challenge and difficult assignments. After her successful stint in Times Square she served as the first female Borough Chief of Detectives in NYPD history and was in charge of 500 detectives in Queens from 1997–99.

An excellent teacher and speaker, Perlov traveled all over the country talking about police work. It was at one of her speaking engagements at Harvard that she met Jane Swift who was then running for lieutenant governor of Massachusetts. Months later she would receive a page at work to "call the governor's office in Massachusetts" and recalls thinking "did we arrest the governor's kid or something?" The page from the Massachusetts governor's office would change her life forever.

Jane Swift had won the election for lieutenant governor and had not forgotten about the excellent speaker with years of experience as a street cop and a manager. She and the new governor offered Perlov the job of Secretary of Public Safety for the state of Massachusetts. As secretary, she would be responsible for overseeing 21 agencies, boards and commissions including the Massachusetts State Police, the Department of Correction, the National Guard, the Department of Fire Services, and the Emergency Management Agency. After talking it over with her husband (a detective lieutenant with the NYPD at the time), she accepted the job.

In her two years as secretary she learned much and made valuable contributions. But she missed being a cop. She wanted to hear the "calls coming over the radio" and the everyday excitement which was part of real police work.She also discovered that she was not a politician which she saw as being a "blood sport" in Massachusetts. She saw the ad for police chief in Raleigh, North Carolina, applied for the job, and was selected (J. Perlov, personal communication, December 13, 2005).

It has been five years since becoming chief of police and Perlov could not be happier. "People respect the police here and respect each other." Her three initial concerns about taking the job – being Jewish, a woman, and from New York – never meant anything.

Perlov leads the police department as part of a team and surrounds herself with good people. She sees police work as involving "three Cs – Cops, Crime, and Community." Being the only Jew in a police department of 725 sworn officers does not bother her. Being chief allows her to do what she feels all Jews should do – Tikkum Olam – repairing the world (J. Perlov, personal communication, December 13, 2005).

Elliot Spitzer

The Attorney General for the State of New York was born on June 10, 1959 to observant Austrian-born Jewish parents in the Riverdale section of the Bronx. He is a graduate of Horace Mann School, and attended Princeton University and Harvard Law School. At Harvard he became the editor of the Harvard Law Review. At Harvard Law, he also met and married Silda Wall and they now have three daughters, Elyssa, Sarabeth and Jenna.

After graduating law school, Spitzer clerked for Judge Robert W. Sweet in Manhattan, then joined the law firm of Paul, Weiss, Rifkind, Wharton & Garrison. He stayed at the firm for about two years before joining the staff of Manhattan District Attorney Robert M. Morgenthau where he spent six years investigating and prosecuting organized crime. One of his biggest cases was in 1992, when Spitzer led the investigation into the Gambino organized crime family's control of Manhattan's trucking and garment industry. He left the DA's office in 1992 to join the law firm of Skadden, Arps, Slate, Meagher & Flom, where he worked until 1998 when he was elected as New York Attorney General.

As Attorney General, Spitzer has taken up civil actions and criminal prosecutions of white-collar crime. "White-collar crimes" are business crimes such as fraud, bribery, insider trading, embezzlement, computer crime, medical crime, public corruption, identity theft, pension fund crime, occupational crime, and forgery. He has pursued these traditional federal jurisdiction matters while maintaining his office's obligation to investigate local cases involving fraud and consumer protection.

Spitzer's approach has often been to seek settlements and plea deals from prospective defendants. His investigations of public corporations has at times been enough to drive down stock prices of the corporation in question. The prospects of an investigation by the Attorney General's office has led corporations facing civil action to choose to settle, and suspects in criminal investigations to seek plea bargains. Spitzer's supporters have lauded his use of this tactic as an innovation in dealing with white collar crime.

One such settlement was the Global Settlement in 2002, where Spitzer sued several investment banks for inflating stock prices, using affiliated brokerage firms to give biased investment advice and "spin" initial public offerings of stock by offering them to CEO's and other influential members of the business community. The resulting settlement was $1.4 billion in compensation and fines paid by the brokerages and investment banks; new rules and enforcement bodies created to govern stock analysts and IPO's; and the insulation of brokerage firms from pressures by investment banks.

The Music Royalty Settlement in 2004 was a similar type of settlement resulting from an investigation of the music industry's practices of keeping hold of royalties instead of paying them to the recording artists. Spitzer's office uncovered $50 million in such royalties owed to musicians whose record labels had failed to keep in contact with them. He reminded label executives that under New York State's Abandoned Property Law, those royalties not being sent to their rightful owners would have to be surrendered to the state.

The participating companies in the settlement included Sony Music Entertainment; Sony ATV Music Publishing; Warner Music Group; UMG Recordings; Universal Music; EMI Music Publishing; EMI Music North America; BMG Songs; Careers-BMG Music Publishing; BMG Music and the Harry Fox Agency. Prominent artists who were owed royalty payments included: David Bowie, Dolly Parton, Harry Belafonte, Liza Minnelli, Dave Matthews, Sean Combs and Gloria Estefan.

As a result of this agreement, new procedures were adopted to ensure that the artists and their descendants will receive the compensation to which they were entitled. In addition, each company agreed to have the heads of the royalty, accounting and legal departments meet regularly to review the status of royalty accounts and take steps to improve royalty payment procedures.

In 2005, Spitzer's office investigated the illegal compensation of radio stations for playing certain songs and deals for disc jockeys to receive gifts from promoters in exchange for playing the songs a certain number of times during the day. In this "Payola Settlement," Spitzer obtained agreements with Sony BMG Music Entertainment and Warner Music Group to put an end to such practices.

On December 7, 2004, Spitzer announced his intention to seek the Democratic nomination for the 2006 election for Governor of New York. His main competitor for the nomination has always been fellow Democrat Senator Charles Schumer, however, Schumer announced that he would not run for Governor, instead accepting an offer to sit on the powerful Finance Committee and head the Democratic Senatorial Campaign Committee.

Spitzer has gained the respect of Democratic leaders nationwide. At a fundraiser held in June 2005, Bill Richardson referred to Spitzer as the "future of the Democratic Party."

Sources

Burke, K. (2005). *Personal Communication* (November 15, 2005).

Claussen-Rogers, N.L. & Arrigo, B.A. (2005). *Police Corruption and Psychological Testing*. Durham, N.C.: Carolina Adademic Press, 2005

Durk, D. (2006). *Personal Communication* (January 30, 2006).

Durk, D. (1976). *The Pleasant Avenue Connection*. New York: Harper and Row.

Gardner, J. (1996). *Crusader: The Hell-Raising Police Career of Detective David Durk*. New York: Random House.

Gelfand, E. (2006). *Personal Communication* (January 10, 2006).

Jaffe, J. (2004). *Personal Communication* (April 10, 2004).

Jaffe, J. (2005). *Personal Communication* (October 10, 2005).

Lardner, J. and Reppetto, T. (2000). *NYPD, A City and its Police*. New York: Henry Holt.

Miller, N. (1992). *Theodore Roosevelt: A Life*. New York: William Morrow & Co.

Safir, H. (2004). *Personal Communication* (March 10, 2004).

Schimmel, G.. (1960). *Joan Palmer, Policewoman*. New York: Dodd, Mead & Co.

Schimmel, G. (2005). *Personal Communication*. (December 10, 2005).

Seedman, A.A. (1971). *Chief!* New York: Arthur Fields Books, Inc.

Seedman, A. (2005). *Personal Communication* (November 12, 2005).

The Jewish Forward, January, 1993

http://crimelibrary.com/serial_killers/predators/kitty_genovese/2.html

http://observer.com/printpage.asp?iid=120623dic=special+news+story+3

http://time.com/time/archive/13July1970

http://time.com/archive/18Sept1972

Chapter 5

California

Emil Harris

Emil Harris was born in Prussia on December 29, 1839. In 1853, along with his aunt, he came to the United States where some members of his family had already settled. After living in New York City for a while, he moved to California where he also had relatives.

In San Francisco his intention was to learn the printing trade and he actually began to work in this field, but the work did not appeal to him and he soon left. He was employed for a while as a waiter in a Kearny Street restaurant and later in his uncle's Stockton billiard hall. He and his uncle also founded a cigar business together. Two years later, Harris' uncle purchased a billiard hall in Visalia, California and Harris managed the establishment until it was sold. He became a naturalized citizen of the United States on March 18, 1867.

In *Emil Harris: Los Angeles Jewish Police Chief*, Norton B. Stern and William M. Kramer discuss how on April 9, 1869, Harris arrived in Los Angeles where he was employed as a bartender at the Wine Rooms on Main Street. He wasted no time becoming involved in civic life, and in June 1869, he registered as a voter. Working in the commercial center of the city, he became aware of the need for fire protection. Together with Henry Wartenberg who was a recognized leader in the Jewish community, he successfully organized a fire brigade (called Fireman's Company) with himself as its elected first assistant foreman.

At the end of 1879, Harris was appointed a patrolman with the City of Los Angeles Police Department. In this capacity he developed a reputation as a brilliant detective and investigator.

He became a major figure in the events of Calle de Los Negros and the Chinese massacre of 1871. The Calle de Los Negros was an area of Los Angeles with a significant underworld involving prostitution, gambling, alcohol consumption, violence, and homicides. Its inhabitants included Indians, Mexicans, Caucasians, and Chinese people of less than the highest character.

The "Chinese massacre" seems to have been a race riot triggered by one Robert Thompson, who attempted to steal $7,000 from a Chinese merchant. Thompson was murdered by Sam Yung during the attempted larceny and a veritable riot ensued where more than twenty Chinese people were killed by an angry mob. Officer Harris was among those who made attempts to control the mob and prevent the loss of life and property among the Chinese. He tried to place them in protective custody, but the infuriated mob followed. Cries of "Hang him!" "Hang him!" "Take him from Harris!" "Shoot him," arose in every direction. The officers proceeded safely with their prisoner until their arrival at the juncture of Temple and Spring Streets. Here they were surrounded, and the Chinaman forcibly taken from them . . ." (p. 53).

In his testimony the next day at the Coroner's Inquest, Harris made clear that all of the Chinese killed that day, except for one, were innocent of any wrongdoing and were the victims of a hostile and murderous mob. This, in spite of the testimony of another eyewitness who claimed that "the Chinamen shot at white people, [and] at the officers . . [including] Harris."

Three months after the events in Negro Alley, it became apparent that the Chinese community was aware of Harris's attempts to reveal the truth surrounding the killings and to vindicate the Chinese individuals charged with crimes. He was given a present in the name of the community by the Wing Chong company consisting of beautiful Chinese embroidery. The gift was a testimonial of their appreciation of his valiant and honest services "from time to time."

"From time to time" was a euphemism for the Chinese massacre of 1871. Harris was one of a small minority who understood and appreciated that the dangers of lawlessness and racism were much greater than any so-called Yellow Peril.

One of the most famous bandits in southern California history was Tiburcio Vasquez who had a frightening reputation for murder and robbery. In April 1874, Sheriff William R. Rowland of Los Angeles

County learned that Vasquez might be in the area, so he assembled a posse comprised of some of the most trustworthy citizens available who were also endowed with physical strength and marksmanship. This posse included police officer Emil Harris.

The lawmen composing the posse were successful in the capture of Vasquez and all become somewhat famous. San Francisco's *Alta California*, the leading newspaper of the day, wrote of Harris' part in the capture of the outlaw.

"Harris was one of Vasquez's captors, and stood his hand with coolness and courage, ready to go for that notorious bandit on a short call. He took, with the others, strong chances for his life; but strategy secured the robber without loss of blood. The fact that he was there and ready with his rifle to do his part, redounds to Harris' credit" (p. 55).

In later years Harris came to regard his part in the Vasquez capture as one of the most interesting parts of his professional life. In fact, he retained the outlaw's rifle in his personal possession.

Harris's satisfaction over his actions in capturing Vasquez were short-lived as just over a week after this event the Committee on Police of the Los Angeles City Council recommended that he be dismissed from the force for having been out of the city "without consent, as required to be obtained by ordinance, and had disobeyed the orders of the Marshal . . . ." It was Harris' expertise as a detective that apparently got him into trouble, for as in the Vasquez case in which he had been deputized by the county sheriff and thus was absent from his city police duties, he was frequently called upon by other law enforcement agencies, including the United States Marshal's office for service in various geographical areas outside of Los Angeles. His supporters on the city council defended him and the charges were quietly dropped.

Harris' reputation continued to build. The *Star* reported: "He has detective qualities second to no man in the State; is brave, cool and energetic and just the man to have associated is such a hazardous undertaking [as the Vasquez affair]" (April 5, 1874, p. 4).

The Los Angeles Police Department during the time that Emil Harris was an officer consisted of only six officers operating under the marshal, who was the elected chief of police. They were divided into two watches of three men each. Two were mounted officers. They received one hundred dollars per month salary while the four patrolman received eighty dollars a month (p. 66).

In the Los Angeles of the 1870s, Harris seemed to know every crook and lawbreaker among the citizenry. The population was under 10,000 people and Harris utilized his firsthand knowledge of people to make arrests quickly. When one Charles Norton's house was broken into, Officer Harris was given the case and "captured his man in five minutes." Once, upon investigating a burglary at a German school-house, Harris learned that a group of young boys were the burglars. Rather than arrested the lads, Harris left the boys to their parents for proper punishment. The police were promised that every stolen article would be replaced in good condition.

Harris saw his share of violence. One night in 1873 he was taking two men to jail when he was attacked by two other men who were apparently comrades of the prisoners. Fortunately for Harris it was only four against one and as the *Star* reported it, "Four men [were soon] on their way to jail surrounded by Officer Harris." When one Richard Stillwell drew a knife on Harris, resisting arrest, Harris tried to take the weapon from him but met with even greater resistance and an assault. "Officer Harris . . .in order to save himself shot Still-well, the ball passing through the muscles of the left arm, in a slanting position, and entering his body . . .the wounded man was then deprived of the knife" (September 17, 1874, p. 3).

On September 29, 1874, the *Star* began to print a series of announce-ments: "For City Marshal – Detective officer Emil Harris desires to announce himself as a candidate for our next City Marshal." Although Harris was a local police officer, by this point in time he was known statewide as an exceptional lawman and a brilliant detective. The San Francisco *Alta* wrote: ". . . Emil Harris is up for the office of City Marshal of that flourishing city . . . Los Angeles cannot do better than reward him with the office of Marshal."

Harris ran for Marshal on the Citizen's Ticket but lost to John J. Carrillo who had received most of the Latin vote of Los Angeles, thus giving him the election. He continued in police work after his defeat at the polls. In 1875 he became a Los Angeles County deputy sheriff and was described as "an able and efficient officer."

In 1877, the title of city Marshal was changed to that of chief of police. That same year the city council voted that the office should be appointed rather than elected and Harris was appointed chief of police on December 27, 1877.

It was a monumental feat for a Jew to become chief of police. But it was even more amazing that Jews were occupying several high offices in the city. In late 1978, an Anglo-Jewish publication of Chicago reported:

"The following co-religionists hold municipal office in Los Angeles, California: Emil Harris, chief of police; Isaiah M. Hellman, city treasurer; Charles Prager, [county] supervisor; Mr. Bernard Cohn is running for mayor and Samuel Prager is running for Tax collector. Just think of it, all of them Jews!" (August 4, 1877, p.3)

One of Chief Harris' first official actions was to put an end to abuses committed by former police officers who retained their police badges after discharge from the force. He did this by replacing the star worm by current police officers with a shield, and by making these new shields the property of the police department and needing to be returned upon discharge from police service. For his own badge, the city council presented him with a gold shield bearing the inscription "Los Angeles Chief of Police" on the front and "Presented to E. Harris by his friends – Los Angeles, Feb. 14, 1878" on the reverse.

Harris initiated several actions in Los Angeles with the aim of reducing crime. First he asked the city council for an ordinance enabling him to control the opium dens that had sprung up in various parts of the city. These dens had become associated with all kinds of crime and deviant behavior. He also restricted the operations of houses of prostitution, cleared sidewalks of debris, removed streetcar rails that obstructed traffic, collected bond money from prisoners seeking release from jail, collected business license fees, enforced sanitary and health ordinances, removed illegally stored gunpowder and ammunition, investigated areas known for attracted criminal elements, and enforced ordinances dealing with cruelty to animals.

Harris sought continually to present a professional image for his officers and himself. He changed the location and furnishings of the police department to allow for a more professional appearance and needed privacy. He arranged for needed repairs to be made to the jail and insured that necessary blankets were available for all prisoners and that a "female cell" be created in the jail which had a window.

Every month the chief of police was required to report a breakdown of crime statistics to the city council. At the end of January 1878, his report included: six misdemeanor arrests, two for assault and battery, four for battery, one for assault, eleven for petty larceny, twelve for drunkenness, two for fast driving, three assault with deadly weapons, one for grand larceny, twelve for trespassing, one for insanity, two for resisting arrest, five for vagrancy, one for indecent exposure, two for cheating, and one for burglary. A total of $758.50 was reported stolen, of which $618.00 was reported recovered.

By the end of 1878 there were major changes occurring in the government of Los Angeles. Every member of the city council was replaced following the election of December 2, 1878 and almost every city official was now out of office. Mayor Frederick A. MacDougall had died, and Councilman Bernard Cohn, who had nominated Harris for the position of chief of police, "was unanimously elected Mayor pro tem to fill the vacancy . . . ." In the closing weeks of their terms, Los Angeles had a Jewish chief of police and a Jewish mayor. This was the first and last time a Jew was to hold either office in the city of Angels.

When the all-new city council voted on a chief of police in 1879, Harris received only two out of fourteen votes and was succeeded by the blacksmith, Henry King as chief of police. Harris continued to work in law enforcement after leaving the police department. He was deputized for special duties such as transporting prisoners to San Quentin prison.

In March 1879 Harris opened a private detective agency and appears to have been one of the first professionally trained and experienced peace officers to become a private investigator following release from public service. As a private detective he handled business cases, served papers for attorneys, conducted a merchant's patrol, and acted as a notary. On occasions he was deputized so that he could make an official, rather than a citizen's arrest, when taking into custody a suspect allegedly guilty of a criminal act against one of his clients. He also kept up his skill as a marksman, and in 1882 won first prize in a Winchester rifle shooting match.

Throughout his life, Harris was involved with the Jewish community. He became one of the prime movers in the establishment of the Young Men's Hebrew Association in Los Angeles, whose active members included some of the most prominent young Jewish figures in the city. He was an active supporter of the first Jewish orphan's home on the west coast. He was also an early and prominent member of Congregation B'nai B'rith (later known as the Wilshire Boulevard Temple).

Emil Harris died on April 28, 1921 at age eighty-two. He was referred to by the newspapers of the time as one of the best known peace officers in Southern California.

Michael Berkow

The son of a Jewish doctor, Michael Berkow pursued a career in law enforcement rather than medicine. His career began in the Rochester, New York, Police Department where he served in a variety of assignments ranging from patrol, to the chief's staff, to narcotics investigations. He also served as the co-commander of a joint police-FBI investigative task force. He left Rochester to serve with the United States Department of Justice as an international police assistance project manager. In this capacity he served as Director of the effort to rebuild the Somalia National Police Force and was the first director for the Haitian National Police Project, where he helped to create the first civilian police force in Haiti's history. Berkow was also in charge of all police training and assistance in South and Central America.

In returning to domestic policing, Berkow assumed command of the Coachella, CA police department where he was credited with leading the department to a major reduction in crime—over 60% in two years—and reorganizing the department to facilitate the adoption of a neighborhood oriented policing strategy. He subsequently became the chief of police in South Pasadena, where he helped the city to become a leader in police related technology and formed true partnerships between the police force and the community.

He then moved on to become Chief of Police of the Irvine Police Department. During his tenure in Irvine he completely re-organized the police department creating a shift to a geographic model of policing closely aligned to the various neighborhoods of the city. In this model, the same supervisors and officers are assigned to a given area.

"He brought a degree of education and sophistication to the job that gave our police department a real boost just when it needed it," said Mayor Larry Agran. "He was very well liked in the general community and certainly among the police officers because he works so hard."

In leaving Irvine, Berkow said of the department, "Irvine reaffirmed the overriding commitment in the men and women who choose to be in policing, that there really is a deep sense of service and altruism in people who serve. I've seen that here in spades" (Agran, 2003).

In his career, Berkow has served as a member of the board of directors for the Police Executive Research Forum and was the 1999 recipient of a prestigious Eisenhower Exchange Fellowship to study the conflict in Northern Ireland and the Royal Ulster Constabulary. He also served as the police liaison for President Jimmy Carter's election monitoring mission to Jamaica in 1997 and 2002, as well as providing anti-corruption training for police forces in Bulgaria, Hungary and Romania. More recently, he has been instrumental in providing civil disorder management training to the Tanzania Police Force in Moshi, Tanzania.

He holds a B.A. in sociology from Kalamazoo College in Michigan, a J.D. from the Syracuse University College of Law and a Masters from Johns Hopkins University where he is a graduate of the Police Executive Leadership Program. He is a graduate of the FBI National Academy and the FBI National Legal Institute.

In April, 2003 Berkow was sworn in is a Deputy Chief of Police for the Los Angeles Police Department to serve under Chief of Police William Bratton. His initial assignment has been as commanding officer of the Professional Standards Bureau with responsibility for all of the anti-corruption and misconduct investigations in the police department.

The *Irvine World News* reported Berkow as saying: "To come into an organization that has that kind of impact on the state, the nation and the world, I'm humbled that I've been asked to come in and do that job. Bratton is a world-renowned leader and outstanding chief. The opportunity to serve with Chief Bratton is very, very appealing" (April 20, 2003).

Berkow is a member of Jewish Institute for National Security Affairs (JINSA) which sponsors official tours for high-level American police and military officials to Israel. In 2002 he participated in one of these tours.

Writing in the *Journal of the International Association of Chiefs of Police*, Berkow stated, "I went with police one night on patrol on Ben Yehuda Street. There was a rock concert that night, about 20,000 people on the street, probably 80 percent 13, 14, 15, 16 years old, the rest parents and toddlers . . . I couldn't imagine a better target." He was amazed that so many people had showed up considering that this is the most bombed street in all of Israel. He realized, however, how important it is for the Israelis that life goes on as usual. He was nevertheless taken aback by what he saw, and this coming from "a guy who lived in Mogadishu for a year" (November, 2004).

While in Israel, Berkow and other police chiefs met with Israeli Minister of Public Security Uzi Landau and National Police Commissioner Shlomo Aharonishsky. They visited sites of bombings at the Dolphinarium nightclub and Hebrew University on Mount Scopus. They also met with the general manager of Azrieli Towers in Tel Aviv, the tallest buildings in the Middle East, which have faced – and thwarted – several attempted terrorist attacks since 2000.

Berkow has also worked for the Justice Department leading police training projects in Somalia and Haiti, and consulting with the national police forces of Jamaica, Northern Ireland, Hungary, and Romania. Regardless of his experience, he and the other Southern California police officials on the trip said that they have already begun applying what they learned in Israel to prepare for possible terrorist attacks in their respective jurisdictions.

Sheriff William "Bill" Kolender

"That's a gentile's job!" This is how Kolender's father reacted to his twenty-year-old son's decision to enter police work. Being a cop was the last thing expected of an orthodox Jew on the south side of Chicago in 1955. But he needed a job and the pay was decent, so he packed up his bags and moved to San Diego California. He became a patrol officer with the San Diego police department and remained there, eventually becoming the chief of police at the age of 40—one of the youngest big city police chiefs in the nation (W. Kolender, personal communication, December 16, 2005).

Some horrific events have occurred in San Diego while Kallender was at the helm of the police department. One of these took place on December 7, 1987 when Pacific Southwest Airlines Flight 1771 crashed in San Luis Obispo killing all 43 people on board including the man who caused the crash, a disgruntled airline employee.

The employee, David Burke had recently been terminated for petty theft and sought his revenge by destroying the flight with himself on it. He apparently purchased a ticket on a Pacific Southwest Airlines Flight. Using his un-surrendered employee credentials, Burke, armed with a loaded .44 Magnum pistol that he had borrowed from a co-worker, was able to bypass the security checkpoint at Los Angeles International Airport. After boarding the plane, Burke wrote a message on an air-sickness bag. The note read "Hi Ray. I think it's sort of ironical that we ended up like this. I asked for some leniency for my family. Remember? Well, I got none and you'll get none." Ray referred to Ray Thompson, who was Burke's supervisor who had terminated him, and was on the flight.

As the plane, a four engine British Aerospace 146-200, cruised at 22,000 feet over San Diego, Burke left his seat and headed to the lavatory, dropping the note on Thomson's lap. As he exited the lavatory a few moments later, Burke took out his handgun and fired twice at Thomson, as the cockpit voice recorder later confirmed. He then opened the cockpit door. A female, presumed to be a flight attendant, told the cockpit crew that "we have a problem." The captain replied, "What kind of problem?" Burke then appeared at the cockpit door and announced "I'm the problem," simultaneously firing three more shots that probably killed the pilots.

Several seconds later, the cockpit recorder picked up increasing windscreen noise as the airplane pitched down and began to accelerate. A final gunshot was heard and it is speculated that Burke fatally shot himself. The plane then descended towards the hillside of a cattle ranch at 4:16 p.m. in the Santa Ana Hills near Templeton, California.

San Diego North Park–based Engine Company 14 was parked at Morley Field on the northern edge of Balboa Park. Four members of the company (one truck) were exercising along Upas Street when the driver heard a huge popping noise. It made him jerk his head around and look up into the sky. He saw the aftermath of the midair collision of the PSA flight with a small Cessna plane. Pieces of the Cessna's propeller were embedded in the right wing of the 727. The impact ruptured fuel and hydraulic lines, causing a massive explosion.

It was determined several days later by the FBI (after the discovery of both the handgun containing six spent bullet casings and the note written on the air-sickness bag) that Burke was the person responsible for the crash. In addition to the evidence uncovered at the crash site, other factors surfaced: Burke's co-worker admitted to having lent him the gun, and Burke had also left a farewell message on his girlfriend's telephone answering machine.

Strict federal laws were passed after the crash, including a law that required "immediate seizure of all airline employee credentials" upon termination from an airline position, and another policy that was put into place where all members of any airline flight crew, including the captain, were to be subjected to the same security measures as are the passengers.

Another event took place on July 18, 1984 in the community of San Ysidro. On that day, an unemployed 41-year-old security Guard named James Oliver Huberty, walked into a McDonald's and began shooting. Armed with a nine-millimeter Uzi carbine (the primary weapon fired in the massacre), a Winchester pump-action twelve-gauge shotgun, and a nine-Millimeter Browning semi-automatic pistol, Huberty killed 21 people, including five children and six teenagers, and wounded 19 in his 77 minute rampage before he was shot and killed by San Diego police sniper Chuck Foster.

Kolender forever remembers that day in July. After the incident, he ordered the formation of a full-time SWAT team which could respond to any similar events in the future. He changed the procedure that the police department used when responding to shootings of this sort, and included psychologists who would counsel survivors, the victims' families, and police officers. When another gunman fatally shot 23 at a restaurant in Killeen, Texas in 1991, San Diego's counseling team was called for help.

The importance of community policing was becoming more and more important during the 1980s and 90s. In March 1982 the *Atlantic Monthly* published an article by James Q. Wilson and George L. Kelling describing the necessity for an "informal control mechanism of the community." The article described the importance of foot patrols which made neighborhoods safer by keeping an eye on strangers, making sure that certain disreputable local citizens observed the rules, and resolving conflicts as they arose on the streets.

In the book *Character and Cops,* Edwin J. Delattre stresses how community policing relies on the police maintaining order by reinforcing the informal control mechanisms of the community itself. He writes that one of the major jobs of a police department . . . is to help people who live in proximity but are in every other respect fragmented by linguistic and other barriers to create and implement the informal social controls that turn fragmented residency into a community (p. 65).

The San Diego section of City Heights is an example of a place which has been benefited from community policing. The residents of City Heights have been traditionally estranged from one another by language and culture and the fact that many of them are illegal aliens. The City Heights Neighborhood Alliance joined with a team of police officers and community organizers to help solve drug-related crimes and provide residents with the awareness and skills needed to solve problems on their own.

In the "Mind Your Own Business is Bad Advice" program instituted by the Mid-City Division of the San Diego Police Department, the alliance between the police and the community helped residents to trust one another to the point where they could intervene for the good of all. In this program, police brought residents together for a common cause, to learn how to interact with the police, and to mobilize efforts to control crimes such as vandalism, prostitution, drug dealing, and loitering. In San Diego, as elsewhere, the informal types of social controls instituted by such community policing programs, helped to decrease crime (especially drug-related) and to increase community morale.

After retiring from the San Diego police department, Kolender served as the Director of the California Youth Authority (CYA), an appointment made by Governor Pete Wilson on September 23, 1991. The California Youth Authority is the largest youth correctional agency in the nation. Prior to his appointment as Director of the Youth Authority, Kolender served as Assistant to the Publisher of the Union-Tribune Publishing Company, which publishes the San Diego Union-Tribune in California's second largest city.

Kolender became the 28th Sheriff of San Diego County on January 2, 1995 and was reelected twice. He is now in his third term until January 2007. Kolender provides leadership to 4,000 employees, including sworn and civilian support personnel, and he oversees a budget of approximately $475 million. As the Sheriff, he is responsible for three main services—law enforcement, detentions, and courts. The Sheriff's Department provides law enforcement to the unincorporated areas of the County, as well as to nine contract cities. There are seven detention facilities operated by the Sheriff and eleven separate court facilities.

During Kolender's term as sheriff he has continued to be taxed with dealing with some of the strangest events and investigations in the country. One of these took place on March 26, 1997 when thirty-nine bodies were found in a rented mansion in the upscale San Diego community of Rancho Santa Fe, California. The victims were all reported to be between 18 and 24 years old and were found all lying in a prone position, hands at their side as if asleep. The men were wearing dark pants and tennis shoes, and there were no signs of trauma or blood. Kolender's deputies described the deaths as a mass suicide.

The Rancho Santa Fe estate is a community that was described as the Beverly Hills of San Diego. It had a swimming pool and tennis court, and was for sale for 1.6 million dollars. The group was called "Heaven's Gate" but had been known by various names over the twenty-two years of its existence. Members referred to themselves simply as "the group," and their leaders as "The Two" or "Bo and Peep." The leaders real names were Marshall Herff Applewhite and Bonnie Lu Nettles.

The group had apparently become involved in a private world of vision, dreams, and paranormal experiences that included contacts with space beings who urged them to abandon their worldly pursuits. They came to believe that there were extraterrestrials who offered humans yet another chance to move to a higher evolutionary level.

For the group, the coming of Comet Hale-Bopp signaled that a heavenly space craft positioned behind the comet was waiting to take them to the next level. The time was apparently ripe to leave their earthly "vessels" by committing suicide.

Another major incident occurred on March 5, 2001 when a ninth grade student at Santana High School in Santee, killed two fellow students and wounded at least 13 in a murderous shooting rampage. One of the victims was found dead at the school, while a second, a 15-year-old boy, died at nearby Grossmont Hospital. Three adults were among the 13 wounded. The school has about 1,900 students and 80 faculty and staff.

According to the *San Diego Union Tribune*, the young boy was smiling when he emerged from a restroom with a long-barreled gun. "He was looking around, smiling, with his weapon. He fired two more shots and went back in," a fellow student reported. Another student said he ran into the bathroom with a security guard after hearing what sounded like a firecracker or a gunshot. "He pointed the gun right at me, but he didn't shoot," the student said. As he and the guard ran out, the gunman shot the guard in the back (March 6, 2001, A-1).

Some students described the scene as "complete chaos." "Everyone scrambled," added another student, "Everybody was running. A whole lot of people were crying. Nobody knew what really happened." She said there was a girl nearby with "blood all over her arm" and another with blood on her hand." Then all of a sudden, we heard more shots going off," she said. "It sounded more like a cap gun than anything. It was really scary. Everybody was running" (March 6, 2001, A-1).

The school provided counseling for students, parents and teachers at the nearby church. President Bush offered his condolences "to the teachers and the children whose lives have been turned upside-down right now." Bush called the shooting "a disgraceful act of cowardice," adding, "When America teaches our children right from wrong and teaches values that respect life in our country, we'll be better off." But, he said, "First things are first. And our prayers go out to the families that lost a child today" (March 6, 2001, A-1).

Over the course of his career, Kolender served as appointee of the Governor on the California Board of Corrections, two terms for the Governor as a Commissioner on the State of California's Commission on Peace Officer Standards and Training (POST), serving as Chair for the year 2001-02; board member of the International Association of Chiefs of Police (IACP) past president of the Major City Police Chiefs' Association; Chairman of the Task Force that integrated the San Diego City Schools; past president of the San Diego Police Officers' Association; and the California Council on Criminal Justice (CCCJ), among others. He also served for eight years on the California Community Colleges Board of Governors and as their president.

Kolender has received many honors over the years, including: the 2004 Courageous Leadership Award by the San Diego Regional Chamber of Commerce; the prestigious John M. Penrith Award for "Excellence in Law Enforcement Administration," given by the alumni and foundation of the National Executive Institute in June 1999; the Neil Morgan Award by LEAD San Diego in May 1999 for exemplary leadership; "Outstanding Alumnus" from San Diego State University in 1985; the Urban League's "Equal Opportunity Award" in 1981; the Golden Man and Boy Award in 1984; and the "Diogenes Award for Truth and Honesty in Government" from the San Diego Chapter of the Public Relations Society of America in 1978.

Kolender is known as a sheriff who believes in early intervention especially in preventing violence and crimes in the schools. He feels that collaboration is needed between teachers, parents, and law enforcement. "We have to help the schools to identify children that they perceive to have problems . . . I think any kindergarten teacher can tell you after a couple of weeks which one of these kids is headed down the path . . . " says Kolender. As sheriff of the third largest county in the country, Kolender is responsible for the care and control of 170,000 adult inmates under his stewardship. He also provides for their mental health needs, which he sees as being instrumental towards rehabilitation. He is particularly involved in the mental health care of juvenile inmates and is amazed how many of them have grown up without anyone ever caring about them "or holding their 'tuchases' responsible" for their behavior (W. Kolender, personal communication, December 16, 2005).

Kolender feels a deep sense of commitment to all of his deputies and civilian staff. He tells every new recruit "take your job seriously but don't take it home." He makes it a point to personally call every single deputy who has experienced a tragedy in his life and makes available to them confidential psychological counseling. Kolender believes that law enforcement personnel should operate at the highest level of ethics and has top officers and civilians in the Sheriff's Department taking ethics courses. He sees the foundation for what his people do being "honesty, fairness, trust and integrity." In 2003, the Jewish community of San Diego County suffered deep emotional losses when wildfires destroyed important components of the Chabad Hebrew Academy and headquarters. Of more than 1,000 homes that were consumed countywide, nearly two dozen, and probably more, were believed to belong to members of the affiliated Jewish community.

In an effort to save religious treasures Chabad staff frantically grabbed three sefer Torahs to protect them from destruction. Everything else in the temporary school trailers was destroyed, including files, materials teachers had collected over a lifetime of teaching, and important Jewish items such as tefillin and tallisim. Also destroyed was a large collection of art prints from the 16th to 19th century, that recently were donated to Chabad, so they were not yet insured.

Sheriff Kolender, along with other public officials, played a vital role in assisting the Jewish community both during the fire and its aftermath. For one thing, Kolender helped coordinate law enforcement in the unincorporated areas of San Diego county, which did not have regular law enforcement. Rabbi Arthur Zuckerman of Congregation Bath Am worked closely with the Sheriff's Department and others, by bringing food to emergency personnel on the fire lines. Besides being the rabbi at Beth Am, he also serves as a chaplain for Kolender and the Sheriff's Department.

The major part of Sheriff Kolender's job is to provide for public safety. It is unfortunate that these days the possibilities of another terrorist attack ranks high on his list of concerns, a concern that he does not see as disappearing anytime soon. He recently told a forum on "Jews and

Law Enforcement" at Tifereth Israel Synagogue that in the wake of the Sept. 11, 2001 attacks, "I truly believe I will be dead, so will my children, and my grandchildren will be very old before this hatred is ever over" (W. Kolender, personal communication, December 16, 2005).

The sheriff said that among his fellow law enforcement officers, "there is not one of us who does not believe that something else is going to happen. We do not know when, we do not know where, nor how, but we know something is going to happen."

"We are doing our best to train our people to be alert, to be observant, to have an intelligent system that allows us to know who in fact would be dangerous in this community—we have done that. We have a joint terrorism task force with the Federal Bureau of Investigation, which is second to none in our state in terms of cooperation and collaboration among all the law enforcement agencies.

"Nevertheless," he said, "I am not sure where [the next terrorist attack] will happen, but if you are not worried about it, there is something wrong. You should worry" (W. Kolender, personal communication, December 16, 2005).

Kolender has commented that he was in Israel when he first saw a robot that can blow up bombs under the guidance of law enforcement personnel stationed safely nearby in a mobile monitoring unit. "Today, San Diego law enforcement has similar capabilities."

Robert Wasserman

Robert Wasserman grew up in Boyle Heights, a heavily Jewish neighborhood in southern California. Endowed with a sense of service at an early age, he joined the National Guard in 1949 only by lying about his age (he was fifteen). His brother was a military policeman so he followed the same route and become one as well. After returning from military activation during the Korean War, Wasserman needed a job and thought to himself "I know about being a cop" and applied with the Montabello police department at age nineteen. His father told him that as the only Jew on a police department "you're never going to get ahead," but he was hired even though he was not technically old enough to apply for a civilian gun permit (R. Wasserman, personal communication, December 21, 2005).

During his years with Montabello, Wasserman heard many ignorant comments directed at and about Jews. Once his own partner mentioned something about "those lousy Jews" but followed it quickly with "but you're different Bob." He felt mad inside when he heard ignorant comments such as this and sometimes would say something. But for the most part he said nothing and just considered the source (R. Wasserman, personal communication, December 21, 2005).

Although he always scored highest on the promotional exams, he was passed over many times for these jobs. This all changed when a new chief was hired who "hated Catholics" so much that he promoted Wasserman because he was not one of them. He could never even consider that Wasserman could be a "Jew." This worked out well until later on when Wasserman married a Catholic woman and "then there were problems."

Wasserman rose up through the ranks at Montabello and in 1969 accepted an offer to be chief of the San Carlos police Department. He recalls that the man who hired him had been an American prisoner of war in a German POW camp. He knew that this man had witnessed the holocaust and the terrible things that were done to Jews in the camps. Because of these experiences he seemed understanding and accepting of Jewish people.

Wasserman remained with San Carlos until 1974 when he became chief of the Fremont police department until retiring in 1991. At 71, he is now the mayor of that city. Although Wasserman has never been religious in the formal sense, he has maintained a proud awareness of his origins and his culture. Others are aware of his pride as well. For example, during the six-day war when it was apparent that Israel was victorious, he entered the roll call room to the cheers and applause of other officers who identified with what they saw as a personal victory for him.

He has always been acutely aware of the struggles faced by Jews working in many professions including police work. He chooses not to be bitter, however, and can even be humorous when discussing the harsh realities that Jews have faced. He thinks of the comic Mel Brooks who when asked how he could make light of the behavior of Nazis in the movie *The Producers*, said "when you hate so badly there is nothing you can do with that hate, so you poke fun at it" (R. Wasserman, personal communication, December 21, 2005).

"You have to show them," advises Wasserman to Jews considering a career in police work, show them that you can do the job and can excel at the job. He encourages Jews to enter law enforcement but warns against being typecast into predictable police roles such as "juvenile crime or public relations." He wants Jewish officers to be out there in the trenches with everyone else.

Bonnie M. Dumanis

On January 6, 2003, Bonnie Dumanis became the first woman to serve as the District Attorney for San Diego County. Upon taking office, she inherited a $14-million budget deficit, which she dealt with by implementing a tough fiscal strategy. She also initiated a major reorganization of the Distract Attorney's office, which had not seen such change for almost 30 years. She chose to surround herself with an experienced, competent and diverse management team. Her second-in-command, Assistant District Attorney Jesse Rodriguez, is the highest ranking Hispanic to serve in that office.

Dumanis leads an office of more than 290 attorneys, over 150 investigators, and more than 600 support staff. She is committed to promotions being based on merit and performance and has implemented an employee training and recognition program to assist in this regard.

The San Diego District Attorney's office is responsible for prosecuting all felonies in the county of San Diego and all misdemeanor crimes in the county except those that occur in the Cities of San Diego and Poway. Currently the District Attorney's Office has a 94 percent conviction rate which is one of the highest in the state.

Dumanis, or "Bonnie" as she is known to almost everyone, grew up in a Jewish and Greek neighborhood near Boston. Her parents were blue-collar liberal democrats who would have preferred that she become a public defender rather than a prosecutor. She was always a very religious person and wanted to be a rabbi but women were not allowed to be rabbis in those days.

But she attended Hebrew school, learned all that she could, and was confirmed. In fact most of her early mentors were her Hebrew school teachers and rabbis.

She began her career in the San Diego DA's office as a junior clerk typist. Not satisfied with her job, and having a desire to move ahead and have an impact on the world, she studied law at night and received her law degree from the Thomas Jefferson School of Law in 1976. She originally served as an Assistant District Attorney and prosecutor under former District Attorney Ed Miller. During these twelve years, she tried more than 50 felony jury trials and also led the Metropolitan Homicide Task Force, which investigated and prosecuted several defendants for dozens of murders of young women in San Diego during the early 1980's.

After serving as a judge in the Municipal State Court for four years, she was elected to the San Diego Superior Court. During her tenure on the bench, Dumanis was the prime mover behind the creation of a Drug Court which she sees as her "passion." She believes strongly in holding non-violent offenders accountable but also using a treatment approach which includes the important elements of "compassion and fairness." Such drug courts have become a model for jurisdictions across the country.

She has never forgotten her first job as a clerk-typist in DA's office and keeps a plaque in her office that reads, "The clerk helping in your division today may be your boss tomorrow" (B. Dumanis, personal communication, January 6, 2006).

Besides her dedication to the law and the criminal justice system, Dumanis has always been involved in various community and civic organizations. She is a past president of the Lawyers Club of San

Diego, served on the Board of Directors of the San Diego Bar Association and taught ethics at the University of San Diego School of Law. She has been recognized by the YWCA with their Tribute to Women Award, and has received the California Women in Government Law and Justice Award and the Salvation Army Women's Auxiliary Women of Dedication Award.

Dumanis sees herself as a "regular person" who likes people and likes to talk to them. She says that she is actually a shy person but admits that nobody would believe it. She is honest and straight-forward and does not believe in putting on pretenses. She walks to work every day stopping to talk to the many people approaching her with greetings or questions. She has a particular affinity for under-served populations and the disenfranchised. Once when walking to work she came across two homeless women and began talking to them. One of them looked up from the pavement and asked "are you Ms. Bonnie?" She invited them both to come to the Salvation Army shelter where she volunteers and told them "if you come on over I'll wait on you" (B. Dumanis, personal communication, January 6, 2006).

At the DA's Office she shows this same caring, understanding, and affinity for one-to-one communication. She makes it a policy to meet individually with the relatives of victims in murder cases and stays attuned to any mental health issues they may present. She has struggled with, and overcome, her own mental health issues, and believes in psychiatry, "cognitive-behavioral therapy", and early intervention. Even her subordinates come to her with problems knowing that they will be received in a warm and non-judgmental fashion.

"Fairness and Justice thou shall pursue," the quote from Deuteronomy hangs on her wall and has been a guiding force in her work as a judge and a prosecutor. She also sees her compassion for people as emanating from the Talmud and Judaic teachings as is her acceptance and respect for people and their diversity. Her parents still refer to her as a "nice Jewish girl," which is a compliment she accepts with pride (B. Dumanis, personal communication, January 6, 2006).

Sources

Agran, L. (2003). Chief Berkow Joining LAPD. Irvine World News http://Irvineworldnews.com (acquired November 27, 2005).

Berkow, M. Homeland Security: The Internal Terrorists. *Journal of the International Association of Chief of Police*, November, 2004.

Delattre, E.J. (2002). *Character and Cops*. Washington, DC: AEI Press.

Dumanis, B. (2006). *Personal Communication* (January 6, 2006).

Kolender, W. (2005). *Personal Communication* (December 16, 2005).

Stern, N.B. & Kramer, W.M. Emil Harris: Los Angeles Jewish Police Chief. *Southern California Quarterly*, 1973, LV, 2.

Terror Hits Home (2001). The San Diego Union Tribune. http://pgasb .pqarchiver.com

Wasserman, R. (2005) *Personal Communication.* (December 21, 2005).

http://Irvineworldnews.com/Astories/Mar20/chief.html.

Chapter 6

Special Cases

Harvey Schlossberg

In 1958, Harvey Schlossberg (shield number 16844) became a cop with the New York City Police Department. As he was in college at the time, and contemplating attending graduate school, he felt that this might be a job where he could earn money while he attended to his studies. He didn't know a lot about what the job entailed, he heard that they were recruiting so he figured he would give it a try. He learned that he would have to attend an academy where he would learn how to box and shoot a pistol. Most of all, he knew that he would get paid a salary during this time. He could never have imagined that he would remain with the police department for twenty years.

In his book *Psychologist with a Gun,* Schlossberg recounts the first time he wore his policeman uniform home. "The police are here, what happened?" This is how his mother reacted when she first saw her son in uniform – she didn't even recognize him. He did not even recognize himself when he looked in the mirror. He knew one thing, with that uniform, his badge, and his gun, he felt different. "The first day I wore the uniform of a cop I felt taller than usual" (p. 29).

After earning his bachelor's degree from Brooklyn College, Schlossberg went on for his Master's degree at C.W. Post Collage and his doctorate at Yeshiva University. In 1971, Harvey Schlossberg became the first known police officer in the country to earn a doctorate in psychology while still a police officer in uniform.

In 1972, when Police Commissioner Patrick Murphy heard that one of his officers (a detective by this point) had earned a doctorate in psychology, he asked him to design the nation's first police psychological service unit. In many ways, Schlossberg can be considered the father of modern police psychology in the United States.

The history of psychology applied to police work in this country can be traced back to the experimental psychologist Hugo Munsterberg, who in 1908 advocated for the entry of psychologists into the arena of the law and the courts, thus setting the stage for psychology's contributions to the legal system, the police, and the courtroom for the next 100 years. The psychologist Lewis Terman (1917) administered the Stanford-Binet intelligence test to 30 police and fire applicants in an attempt to set minimum standards for making hiring decisions. He published the results of his efforts in the first issue of the *Journal of Applied Psychology*, finding that the average IQ score of police applicants was 84. Terman then recommended that no police applicant with an IQ score of less than 84 be hired.

"Police psychology" as it would eventually be called, or the application of psychological principles and methods to law enforcement, includes topics such as the screening and hiring of police officers, training, investigations, hostage negotiations, interrogations and confessions, eyewitness testimony, stress counseling, and fitness-for-duty evaluations, among others.

In *Psychologist with a Gun*, Schlossberg outlined his thoughts for a psychological services unit within the police department. He listed the services he saw such a unit providing. They included:

1. The conducting of psychological evaluations, consisting of psychological testing, psychiatric interviews, diagnosis and prognosis, all in an attempt to discover if certain policemen sent to [him] by their superiors or coming to [his] office voluntarily were too emotionally upset to be allowed to carry a gun. If they were found to be, then either short-term or long-term therapy would be recommended and an attempt made to find psychiatrists to treat them.

2. Marriage counseling, where marital problems impaired a policeman's work. Guidance and counseling to police who had minor problems.
3. Referral of families, wives, or children for treatment if they needed it.
4. Psychological testing and evaluation of candidates for promotion.
5. Psychological testing and evaluation of all recruits.
6. Research and operational consultations to other units within the department for personnel selection and research into function.
7. Instructional services to promotion classes on recognition of psychiatric problems commonly encountered by supervisors.
8. Continued administration of a pilot program for certain officers who needed therapy, which would include referral, payment, and supervision of the therapeutic process.
9. Maintaining of liaison with the honorary psychiatrists who served the Medical Division as consultants.
10. Acting as consultant to the district surgeons on psychological matters concerning members of the force.
11. Conducting of special lectures on psychological problems related to special police functions.
12. Representing the department on psychological matters in lectures before lay and professional organizations.
13. Consultant on behavioral patterns in crime situations.
14. Teaching of specialized courses for department units.
15. Acting as liaison with civilian psychiatrists and psychologists and as advisor to them on special problems relating to the demands of police work. (p. 93)

In the psychological screening or police recruits, Schlossberg instituted an assessment battery which included a structured clinical interview along with the administration of certain psychological tests.

These tests included the *Thorndike Dimensions of Temperament Scale*, the *Cornell Medical Index* (CMI), *Edwards Personal Preference Schedule* (EPPS), the *Minnesota Multiphasic Personality Inventory* (MMPI), and the *House-Tree-Person Test* (HTP) (H. Schlossberg, personal communication, February 1, 2006).

The *Thorndike Dimensions of Temperament Scale* was originally published in 1966 and was a self-report inventory through which the individual describes himself with respect to ten dimensions of temperament including: Sociable; Ascendant; Cheerful; Placid; Accepting; Tough-Minded; Reflective; Impulsive; Active; and Responsible.

The *Edwards Personal Preference Schedule* (EPPS) was developed in 1959 based on the manifest need system theory of H.S. Murray and his associates at the Harvard Psychological Clinic. Beginning with 15 needs drawn from Murry's list of manifest needs, Edwards prepared sets of items whose content appeared to fit each need. Examples included the need for Achievement (to do one's best and accomplish something difficult), Deference (to conform to what is expected), Exhibition (to be the center of attention), Intraception (to analyze the motives and feelings of oneself and others), Dominance (to influence others and to be regarded as a leader), and Nurturance (to help others in trouble).

The CMI was created in 1949 and was a self-administered health questionnaire developed to obtain details of the medical history as an adjunct to the medical interview. It consisted of 195 questions divided into eighteen sections; the first twelve sections dealt with somatic complaints and the last six with mood and feeling patterns.

The MMPI was developed in the late 1930s by a psychologist and a psychiatrist at the University of Minnesota. The test had ten clinical scales and three validity scales plus various supplementary scales. The clinical scales were intended to distinguish groups of people with psychiatric disorders and has somewhat exotic-sounding names. The names of these primary clinical scales have remained the same for the last 75 years even through a re-standardization process in 1989. The scales include hypochondriasis, depression, hysteria, psychopathic-deviate, masculinity-femininity, paranoia, psychesthenia, schizophrenia, hypomania, social affiliation.

The H-T-P test is a projective technique developed by John Buck and was originally an outgrowth of the "Good enough" scale which was utilized to assess intellectual functioning. In administering the HTP test, the subject is asked to draw alternately a house, a tree, and a person. Buck felt artistic creativity represented a stream of personality characteristics that flowed onto graphic art. He believed that through drawings, subjects objectified unconscious difficulties by sketching the inner image of primary process. Since it was assumed that the content and quality of the H-T-P was not attributable to the stimulus itself, he believed it had to be rooted in the individual's basic personality.

This screening process was designed to insure that only the psychologically fit and "normal" person becomes a police officer. But there is much to suggest that even the most emotionally stable individual "changes" when he becomes a police officer.

On the job the world of the police officer is often very negative as he sees mostly the bad part of society. This may skew the officer's opinions on the character of the average human being and create a cynicism, isolation, and difficulty trusting people in general. Although the stress of viewing many horrific events, violence, and trauma can be substantial in police work, it is made worse by its intermittent nature interspersed with periods of boredom and calm. Officers cannot usually control entrance into most traumatic and dangerous situations they face, they have to react to problems and typically do so without sufficient warning or preparation. Officers are also required to always be in emotional control and must show extreme restraint even under highly emotional circumstances.

Police officers must wear a social mask which they put on with the uniform. Often, what our society expects from police officers is a perfect blend of robot and person. In any confrontation, no matter the potential for violence, you're not supposed to display emotion or the human characteristics that result from adrenaline. People realize officers are human, but they don't understand that they can't be trained to a point where we override every human emotion.

As a result of these stressors, police officers run a greater risk than the general population of developing many stress-related conditions such as hypertension, heart disease, stomach disorders, psychosomatic illnesses, and alcohol and substance abuse. Police officers also experience divorce twice the rate of individuals in other occupations, and have a suicide rate two to six times greater than the national average. In addition, there is research indicating that police work actually "changes people". Despite some popular beliefs that the police are naturally authoritarian, ultra-conservative, or prone to dehumanizing others, officers are more likely to have developed some of these characteristics (if present at all) while on the force.

Because of these factors, Schlossberg knew that it was not enough to psychologically screen police recruits, it would be necessary to provide psychological counseling for them as well. Accordingly, the psychological services unit of the police department offered a full array of individual and group psychotherapy.

Schlossberg knew that for almost all police officers, the "credibility" of anyone offering therapy for officers would be a major issue. Police officers are traditionally very distrustful and wary of an outsider who they perceive as not understanding what the world of a police officer is like. For Schlossberg himself this was not an issue since in addition to being a psychologist he was also a cop. "I ran after bad guys on the same rooftops as they did" he would say (H. Schlossberg, personal communication, February 1, 2006).

Peer counseling, or having cops counsel other cops, was a technique brought to the forefront by Schlossberg. He trained police officers to help other officers in trouble and to be "group leaders" of police group counseling sessions. Interestingly enough, he found that these lay therapist-cops who were leading these groups were often more accurate than Schlossberg himself in spotting the violent-prone officers in the groups.

Schlossberg felt strongly that it was best to catch problems before they developed into nightmares. He instituted what he called an "early warning system" in which certain markers or signals in a policeman's performance would set off a "psychological alarm" of sorts that therapeutic intervention was needed.

He also recommended to the police brass that officers have regular therapy sessions as a means of warding off problems before they grew into bigger ones. A major advantage of such an approach would be to remove the "stigma" of seeing the "shrink" which so often occurs in police work. By making such visits mandatory, the officer's macho self-image could be maintained. Unfortunately, police department higher-ups shot down this idea as taking up too many man hours.

One of the most notable and far-reaching initiatives taken by Schlossberg was his part in developing the nation's first true Hostage Negotiations Team in 1972. As both a psychologist and a police detective, he provided most of the psychological consultation needed in all aspects of team including recruitment of team members and actual negotiating techniques.

In January 1973, New York City police officers interrupted a robbery in progress at Al's Sporting Goods store in Brooklyn. What resulted was a 48-hour siege involving 11 hostages, and four armed men. "In a way, the Brooklyn siege was like a final exam for our hostage negotiations training" (H. Schlossberg, personal communication, February 1, 2006).

The gunmen had barricaded themselves with the hostages inside the store, where they were pinned down by police fire. Around the same time, in a different part of the city, a police car pulled up at Schlossberg's home. "Out I went into the back of the cruiser," he recalls. "The neighbors thought I was getting locked up" (H. Schlossberg, personal communication, February 1, 2006).

One of the first things Schlossberg did when arriving on the scene was to calm things down. He ordered the cops to stop shooting and wait it out. "I didn't want to storm the place, I wanted to talk to them," he recalls. The gunmen had recently sent out a note stating that one of their comrades was injured. They requested medical aid and food. This made Schlossberg believe that these men were more concerned with staying alive than with suicide. He sent in a police radio and initiated a dialogue.

In the end, the hostages escaped by a clever trick: they had persuaded their captures to let them go to the rear of the store in anticipation of a shoot-out. Instead, they broke a plasterboard wall and exited to the roof through a hidden stairway. Schlossberg felt that by basically "doing nothing" and waiting out the situation, the gunmen's alertness relaxed and they fell for the hostages' ruse.

This type of ending suits Schlossberg fine since his philosophy has always been to "be alive and works things out." He would often advise others to "slow down" in their handling of police-related situations which did not require snap decision-making. In his counseling and consultation roles as a psychologist, he would always like to "leave people feeling good" (H. Schlossberg, personal communication, February 1, 2006).

Since retiring from the New York City police department in 1978, Schlossberg has been engaged in the private practice of clinical and forensic psychology. In addition to seeing patients, he consults with and advises police departments all across the country. He is an Associate Professor in the College of Professional Studies at St. John's University and teaches courses in the psychology of terrorism, among others.

Reuben Greenberg

Reuben Greenberg was the tough-talking black Jewish Texan chief of the Charleston South Carolina police department for almost 20 years until his retirement in 2005. What could be more unlikely than a black, Orthodox Jew from Texas transforming a city in the heart of the Confederacy from a crime-ridden center of corruption to a uniquely well-managed place that cracked down on crime at the same time it virtually eliminated police brutality and even rudeness?

From the beginning of his tenure Greenberg told his officers that their job was not to punish (that was up to the courts), but to make arrests, and in order to do that they had to be on good terms with the citizens. Thus, he made it clear that he would fire anyone who used abusive language with a citizen. He wanted his officers to have face-to-face contact with citizens and not be hidden in patrol cars. So he had officers walking beats, riding bicycles, and even riding horses in order to be more visible and available to all people. He also wanted his officers to be educated and insisted that they obtain college degrees.

Chief Greenberg became something of a celebrity. He has been referred to as a "Black, Jewish, Roller-Skating Cop," and even *60 Minutes* featured him as a guest. He was in demand by urban police departments such as New York, Washington and Los Angeles, but was always happy with remaining in Charleston.

In his book *Let's Take Back Our Streets!* Greenberg talks about his childhood and his mixed ethnic background. His father, Sol Greenberg, was a Russian Jew who immigrated to this country from the Ukraine and somehow found his way to Texas. He met and fell in love with a lovely African-American woman. They married and had six children at a time when not only was such a mixed marriage virtually unthinkable, it was illegal. Reuben was born to the family in 1943.

Greenberg's father had little if any identification with being Jewish or with "Yiddishkeit" and changed the family name to "Green" which was the name used by the family in Houston. The Green children were raised as Methodists (Greenberg's mother's religion) and Greenberg did not start using his grandfather's last name until his college days when his identification with Judaism solidified.

Greenberg attended an all black neighborhood school (this was prior to the Supreme Court's decision which desegregated the schools of the south.) He recalls being very touched by the phrase in the Pledge of Allegiance "liberty and justice for all" but knew that it didn't apply to him. But he did not grow up with resentment or hate. Rather he felt awed by the moral and ethical principles which made this country great.

It was during Greenberg's involvement in the civil rights movement of the 1960s that his interests in Judaism were awakened. In
his book he discusses having been impressed with the courage of Jews
on the picket lines who fought for equality despite risks to their careers
and financial security.

After teaching public administration for two years at the University
of North Carolina, Greenberg accepted a position as a Major on the
administrative team of the Chief of the Savannah police department.
It was in Georgia that he attended Agudath Achim, a Conservative
synagogue, and began the serious study of Judaism.

Greenberg was attracted by the survival of the Jewish religion for
thousands of years despite the religion's acceptance of dissent and
spirited disagreements among its adherents. He felt that Judaism had
nothing "to sell" and had no requirements other than belief in a supreme
being and that one lives in peace with others. Although at first associated with the Reform movement in Judaism, Greenberg wanted the
opportunity for more of what he described in his book as a "demanding religious experience." But at the same time he found it difficult to
make the types of commitments necessary for orthodox Judaism. Ultimately he decided to join a conservative congregation, and this is the
branch of Judaism with which he has remained identified to this day.

Greenburg has always been direct with his opinions and he has
some strong feelings about things like drugs, drunk driving, and
"lawyers." In *Let's Take Back Our Streets!*, he talks about an under-
current of hypocrisy which runs through the whole drug enforcement
issue. He says:

> We pass laws making the use or sale of pot illegal, but con-
> trols on our alcohol consumption are pretty lax. The effects
> of two or three martinis are similar to the high someone gets
> from smoking a couple of joints. A youngster may well ask
> himself, "What's the difference?" You've got your favorite
> drug, Dad, and I've got mine. Only difference is, yours is legal
> and mine isn't" (p. 29).

Greenberg feels that we need to turn the attitude towards drugs around and realize that abuse of substances of any form is a big problem. He wants to persuade enough people that using crack or cocaine or heroin is basically stupid. "Demand is the key. Stop, or at least significantly diminish, the demand and you dry up the supply" (p. 30).

Greenberg is particularly incensed about drunk drivers. He feels that harsher treatment and more severe penalties are the answer to this problem. He cites how in Sweden, the first arrest for drunk driving means loss of a divers license. He wants to see harsh penalties for any driver who continues to ignore the law and endanger the lives, hopes, and dreams of others.

> Teach [drunk drivers'] children to regard them with scorn and contempt. Publish their names, regardless of wealth or social position, in headlines of shame. Lock them up and throw away the key. Off with the leads of the drunk drivers (p. 34).

Greenberg also has some strong feelings about lawyers. Just outside the door to his office in police headquarters hung a little framed sign which read:

> The other night a burglar broke into the Broad Street home of a prominent Charleston lawyer. And after a terrific struggle, the lawyer succeeded in robbing him (p. 62).

He admits that he regards many lawyers with "indignation bordering on disgust," and pretty much sees them as "trained liars" who charge too much, use language that is intentionally confusing, and have little respect for justice (p. 63).

Greenberg feels that many lawyers are too worried about "procedures" and not adequately concerned with "justice." He also feels that they are overly concerned with their own reputations rather than doing the right thing. "Losing a big case can damage a prosecutor's reputation. Defense lawyers can lose a dozen and not be hurt at all," he says (p. 65).

But Greenberg's deepest and most personal of emotions are related to his identity of being both black and Jewish. He will never forget the faces of the Ethiopian Jews he saw in Israel. He realized that these people had lived in Africa as Jews for thousands of years, cut off from their fellow Jews, under extremely severe social conditions. But they had been rescued by other Jews and brought to Israel in a series of dramatic airlifts. He recalls, "As I stood there watching them, I was proud, tremendously proud of being what I am – a Jew" (p. 192).

Stephen M. Passamaneck

In February 1976, Dr. Stephen M. Passamaneck came across an article in the *Los Angeles Times* about the Chaplains Unit of the Los Angeles County Sheriff's Department. He can recall wanting to be involved in something that was hands on and not the usual thing. He subsequently became a Chaplain with the Sheriff's Office.

Most of Dr. Passamaneck's law enforcement congregants were not Jewish but that did not diminish neither the quantity or quality of his work as a chaplain. In addition to counseling, debriefing, and sick calls, he was always available to anyone who wanted to talk or for serious incidents.

After serving as a Chaplain for two years at his first station, he was assigned in 1978 to the Sheriff's West Hollywood station where he would continue until 1985. Much of the learning that Passamaneck experienced took place while riding alongside officers on patrol. As a Chaplain he logged over 1500 hours as a ride-along, working in the field.

Early in 1986, Passamaneck concluded that he could better serve the deputies if he took police training. He applied to the Sheriff's Reserve Academy, took the physical and psychological examinations and survived the regular training course as a line deputy. Later he worked as part of a special unit in warrant service and surveillance of some rather dangerous criminals. During this time, while still maintaining his teaching responsibilities and academic writing, he was promoted to Supervising Chaplain in the Department. He even became an expert pistol shot.

Although he retired in 1992 from the surveillance and apprehension unit with the rank of Reserve Captain, he remained active as a Chaplain. His years of distinguished service were recognized when he was awarded the Los Angeles County Sheriff's Department Exemplary Service Medal in 1991. He has also been honored by the Shomrim Society.

In 2003 Passamaneck published *Police Ethics and the Jewish Tradition*, a work of commentary and theory that examines Jewish tradition and law as related to police ethics. He feels that Jewish tradition has a lot to teach about ethics and morality in many fields, with police work being just one.

Dr. Passamaneck has been a member of the International Conference of Police Chaplains (ICPC) since the late 1980s. It was his membership in the ICPC which brought him to the attention of the Port Authority Police Department (PAPD) in New York City on September 12, 2001 with a request for help at Ground Zero. He would spend thirteen-hour days there, alongside emergency crews, police officers, firefighters, construction workers, and other Chaplains in the days immediately following the terrorist attacks.

Stephen Rayow

From 1960 to 1980 Rabbi Stephen Rayow served with the NYPD as a patrolman and a detective. Much of his career was spent in Internal Affairs and he was a special investigator with the Knapp Commission.

Rayow recalls being approached in the police academy as a young recruit and asked if he would perform undercover work as part of an ongoing investigation of uniformed police officers. Needless to say, he was not well-liked by many members of the force. He can recall having been called every name in the book as he performed his duties ridding the department of corrupt and dishonest cops. One time, another officer, "a big Nazi guy," approached Rayow and barked "You know you can't trust these Jews . . . Hitler didn't go far enough." Rayow lifted the man up "with strength that must have come from Hashem" threw him up against the wall and put him on notice about "Jew" comments and "Hitler" comments. He was never bothered by this big brute again (S. Rayow. personal communication, October 1, 2003).

Rayow has seen a lot of resentment towards Jews on the police department during his years and thinks that much of it had to do with jealousy. For example, he states that in the 1960s about 10% of the cops were Jewish but about fifty percent of the high-ranking brass were Jewish. Many non-Jewish cops had problems with these numbers and did not like that so many supervisory positions were held by these "Jewish college boys" (S. Rayow, personal communication, October 1, 2003).

Overall, Rayow sees Jews as a group as having many of the same problems as police officers as a group. Jews stand out, perhaps this is because of their intelligence or accomplishments, and the police stand apart from the average citizen as well. He sees both Jews and the police as kind of like "Rorschach ink blots" in that people tend to project their own fears and internal conflicts onto them.

Rayow once had somewhat of a religious calling which he put on hold during his police career and lived as a secular Jew. But in 1978, he had a spiritual re-awakening and resumed his Jewish studies as an "interested lay person." In 1989, he considered Smicha (Rabbinic ordination) when he met a young Rabbi who was stricken with Leukemia. He became Rayow's mentor and friend and asked him to be his Chazzan (cantor). Shortly before his death he put Rayow in contact with a Rabbi in New York City who had a seminary and training program for both Rabbinical and "interfaith ministers." This appealed to Rayow because of his desire to help in the performance of Tikkun Olam (repair of the world) by furtherance of mutual respect and understanding among all people. In 1995 Rayow was ordained a Rabbi by the Chabad Lubivitch movement.

Shlomo Koenig

In Rockland County New York, Sheriff James Kralik says that the Police Academy had never seen anything like this before – "A guy walks in with a bowler hat on, a beard, a coat coming down to his knees, He looks like something out of 'Fiddler on the Roof'." But this is how Shlomo Koenig first presented for his deputy sheriff academy training.

It was originally Sheriff Kralik's idea that Koenig apply to be a deputy sheriff. While at the academy certain arrangements had to be made. Saturday classes were out for Koenig because of the Jewish Sabbath. Then there was the issue of the beard. Beards are forbidden by the Sheriff's department, and not having a beard is forbidden for Hassidic Jews. Koenig received a waiver.

He took 600 hours of training and graduated with excellent grades. He also earned a shooting award. Carrying a gun presents no ethical problem for Koenig. As for using it, he says "You're not allowed to murder, but self-defense is not murder" (Fitzgerald, 1997, p. 1).

Koenig eventually put on the tan uniform and silver star of a Rockland County Sheriff's deputy. The Sheriff's Office has about 65 full-time officers and several part-time ones like Koenig. "It took a lot of courage," says Kralik. As a deputy Koenig has helped draft guidelines for his fellow officers in dealing with the Hassidic community. Getting a description of a mugger, for example, can be difficult if the victim isn't familiar with secular clothing. A witness might say the mugger wore blue pants, but if asked whether they were blue jeans, "chances are you're going to get a yes, even though there's a 99% chance the person doesn't really know what blue jeans are," Koenig says. "They say yes because people don't want to be caught not understanding" (Fitzgerald, 1997, p. 1).

Then there's the language problem. Many of Rockland County's Hassidic Jews do not speak English well and few police officers know Yiddish. Koenig has put together a collection of useful phrases for deputies to use: "Vas is dan numen?" (What is your name?), "Is ales in ordernung?" (Are you all right?"), "Vi azoi hot er oizgesen?" (What did he look like?).

"I'm a Jew first, a police officer second," says Koenig. "I still try to live on my own in my smaller world. I try to do my studying, my praying, the religious education of my kids. I also try to be a sheriff.

I have to be able to work with society and I try to do that" (S. Koenig, personal communication, October 21, 2004).

As a deputy, Koenig continues to bridge the gap between the Sheriff's Department and Rockland County's growing Orthodox Jewish community. He served as a Yiddish translator or explained the customs of one group to the other. For example, a driver who abandons his car on the highway and begins walking on the shoulder might look suspicious to an officer. But it might just be an Orthodox Jew, late for getting home on a Friday and forbidden to drive after sunset. Or an officer might take offense if a Hassidic woman refuses to take a speeding ticket handed to her. Such contact between the sexes is forbidden – and deputies now put the ticket down so the woman can pick it up.

Deputy Koenig is perhaps the only Hassidic police officer in the nation. He is proud to be both an orthodox Jew and a cop, despite his unusual appearance. He says, "Even in Israel they don't have anything like me" (S. Koenig, personal communication, October 21, 2004).

Cyril H. Wecht

The Allegheny County Coroner until 2006, Dr. Cyril H. Wecht was born in 1931 in a small Pennsylvania coal-mining town with hardly any Jews. He recalls hearing comments people made about Jews and remembers asking his mother at age three, "Did I kill someone named Jesus Christ?" His parents came from Russia and the Ukraine and exerted a strong Jewish and Talmudic influence on him. They also knew firsthand about anti-Semitism and his father cautioned young Cyril to be ever alert. "There are winter anti-Semites and summer anti-Semites" cautioned his father, "the winter ones are covered up with an overcoat." He had a Bar Mitzvah but did not attend Hebrew school primarily because of the massive amount of time he invested in learning and playing the violin. "My violin was my Hebrew School," he states (C. Wecht, personal communication, January 15, 2006).

He eventually moved to Pittsburgh with his parents,where they opened a grocery store. As a youngster he was active in sports, achieved high grades, and always played the violin. But it was made clear to him by his father from the very beginning that he was to become a doctor, or as his father would say "Doctor, doctor, doctor" over and over again. The feeling was that this was the perfect profession for a bright Jewish boy because it made a good living, was prestigious, and you did not have to worry too much about discrimination. It is interesting to note that two of Wecht's four children would became doctors as well.

His curiosity and interest in morgues started at an early age, according to his biography in *Cause of Death*. Wecht and his friends used to go to the city morgue as youths to look around. There were fresh bodies laying behind glass windows as well as autopsied remains. The boys got a good idea what death looked and smelled like.

Wecht received a medical degree from the University of Pittsburgh School of Medicine in 1956. He did his internship at St. Francis General Hospital and Rehabilitation Institute and his residency in pathology at the Veterans Administration Hospital in Pittsburgh from 1957 to 1959. Being interested in legal medicine, he began law school concurrently with his residency after receiving special permission to do so.

Although accepted to Harvard and Yale law school, he decided to attend the University of Pittsburgh because he was offered a full scholarship. As it turned out, however, he finished his last year of law school at the University of Maryland in 1962.

Wecht has held numerous medical and academic appointments. These include being a pathologist for North Charles General Hospital in Baltimore; the director of the Pittsburgh Pathology and Toxicology Institute; the laboratory director of the podiatry hospital in Pittsburgh; and the Chairman of the Department of Pathology of St. Francis Hospital.

He is also an adjunct professor with the Duquesne University John G. Rangos Graduate School of Health Sciences; a clinical professor or pathology with the University of Pittsburgh School of Medicine; and a clinical professor of epidemiology at the University of Pittsburgh Graduate School of Public Health.

Wecht is certified by the American Board of Pathology and is a Fellow of the College of American Pathologists and the American Society of Clinical Pathologists. As a medical expert, he has performed over 14,000 autopsies and has supervised, reviewed or been consulted on approximately 30,000 additional postmortem examinations.

He has served as president of the American College of Legal Medicine and the American Academy of Forensics Sciences. He actively consults on medico-legal investigations and forensic science issues, as well as being a lecturer and author, and teaches the bi-annual course for Certified Medical Investigator for the American College of Forensic Examiners International. Besides giving testimony, Wecht is often a guest on national television and radio shows, and provides expert analyses for breaking stories in newspapers.

Wecht is the author of five books including *Legal Medicine* (1988) *United States Medicolegal Autopsy Laws* (1989), *Cause of Death: The Final Diagnosis* (1994), *Grave Secrets* (1996), *Forensic Sciences* (1997) and *Who Killed Jonbenet Ramsey?* (1998). He has also authored more than 500 professional articles and edited many outstanding professional publications in law and forensic science.

He has always been involved in Jewish causes such as the Jewish Community Relations Council of Pittsburgh, the American Jewish Committee, The Jewish Family and Children's Service of Pittsburgh, the American Jewish Congress, and the Kollel Bais Yitzchok Institute for Advanced Torah Studies. He serves on the board of directors of the Jewish Family Assistance Fund, the Zionist Organization of America, and the Anti-Defamation League of B'Nai B'rith. He has been the recipient of the Jewish National Fund "Tree of Life Award, among others.

Dr. Wecht has been involved in the investigation of numerous high-profile cases. Among these has been the assassination of President John F. Kennedy on November 22, 1963. He was working in the Los Angeles morgue surrounded by corpses when the news broke about the assassination. He would later be one of the medical experts who testified before the House Select Committee on Assassinations in 1978.

During his testimony Wecht argued against the idea that President John F. Kennedy was shot by one gunman from the Texas Book Depository. It was partly as a result of Wecht's testimony that the final report concluded that, on the basis of the evidence available to it, President John F. Kennedy was probably assassinated as a result of a conspiracy.

Wecht has become one of the foremost critics of the Warren Report, and in his 1993 book, *Cause of Death*, he characterized the Report as "absolute nonsense," and and the famous "single-bullet" assertion "an asinine, pseudoscientific sham at best."

After examining the Kennedy autopsy photographs and X-rays, Wecht calculated the angle of the bullet that entered the rear of the President and presumably exited through the hole in the throat. He estimated the angles of the bullet path as 11.5 degrees downward and 17.5 degrees right to left. Both of these angles are incompatible with a shot fired from the sixth-floor southeast corner window of the Texas School Book Depository building. They are also incompatible with a bullet exiting Kennedy's throat and striking Governor Connally. The governor was struck on the right side of his back between the shoulder blade and the armpit. Since he was sitting directly in front of President Kennedy, a bullet traveling downward and right to left could not have struck Governor Connally unless the bullet made a right and then a left angle turn in mid-air.

Wecht calculated that the bullet which exited the president's throat (which has never been proven) would have passed over Mrs. Connally's right shoulder and over the left shoulder of the driver of the limousine, Secret Service Agent William Greer, and then would have struck the grass on the north side of Elm Street. Wecht believes that based on his computation of the angles of the bullet wounds in President Kennedy and Governor Connally, that the shots were fired from a lower floor of the Book Depository building and from the roof of the Dal-Tex Building.

Even though precise angles of the bullet wounds are not known, Dr. Wecht's contention that a bullet fired from the sixth-floor southeast corner window of the Depository building and passing through President Kennedy's neck could not have hit Connally on the right side of his back is strongly supported by the known facts. Excepts of eighteen frames (or one second), of the Zapruder film clearly shows Governor Connally to be seated directly in front of President Kennedy. If a bullet fired from the sixth-floor window entered the rear of Kennedy's neck and exited from the front of his throat, it would have traveled at a right-to-left angle to strike Connally Since the entrance hole on Governor Connally's back was to the right of the alleged exit hole of the bullet from Kennedy's throat, that same bullet could not have struck the governor. Only during that one second, when the street sign blocked Zapruder's view of the limousine, could Connally have been struck by the same bullet. That is possible only under the extremely unlikely circumstance that the governor jumped out of his seat, moved four feet to his left, squatted down, received a shot in the back, then returned to his original position - all within one second. This investigation and circumstances surrounding the assassination have not been completely resolved as of this date.

Although he is not very religious, Wecht's identity as a Jew is one of the most important things to him. He is active in numerous Jewish organizations and has been to Israel six times. In fact, he managed to be present in Israel for the trial of Adolf Eichmann and will never forget the experience.

In 1961, the world watched the first televised courtroom trial as a Jerusalem court tried Eichmann for crimes against the Jewish people. Eichmann's role in deporting the Jews of Europe to concentration camps made him the target of a fifteen-year manhunt by Israeli agents. His defense, like that of other Nazis, was that he was "just following orders."

Israel's Prime Minister David Ben Gurion wanted to broadcast the trial to educate a generation that had come of age after World War II about the atrocities of the Holocaust. The trial was an emotionally explosive event that revealed for the first time to a shocked world audience the Nazi campaign to exterminate European Jewry.

In 1950, Eichmann had fled to Argentina with the help of the Nazi underground. The Israeli government found him living in Buenos Aires with his wife and three sons. In May, 1960, the Israelis kidnapped him and forcibly brought him to Israel to stand trial as a war criminal.

Eichmann was the mastermind behind moving the Jewish people out of their homes into the ghettoes, and then into the concentration camps. He proved to be the Nazi's foremost Jewish specialist. His ability to organize, categorize, and supervise enabled him to bring over six million Jews to their deaths. This was further accomplished by piling millions of men, women, and children in cattle cars to be sent to the death camps.

During the trial, Eichmann sat enclosed within a glass booth. He became known, and is known today, as The Man in the Glass Booth. The Israelis built the booth for his protection because they feared someone would try to kill him before the trial was over.

One of the extraordinary aspects of the Eichmann trial is that no one knew very much about the Holocaust when the trial began. Holocaust survivors did not speak about their ordeals at the hands of the Nazis until the trial. To many, the Holocaust was an unspeakable remembrance, but the trial was a catharsis, and people began to tell their tales. Gideon Hausner, Attorney General representing the State of Israel, called over 100 witnesses to the stand. The courtroom was packed. After an emotional 16 weeks, Eichmann was found guilty on all 15 counts of the criminal indictment against him. He was hanged, his body cremated, and his ashes were scattered in the Mediterranean Sea.

Wecht doesn't understand why many people do not associate "Jew" with law enforcement. He thinks this has something to do with the common notion that "Jews are not supposed to be tough" but are expected to be professionals and make a lot of money. He feels, perhaps with good reason, that many people are only comfortable when Jews are helpless and weak and not when they are strong, "certainly this has been the case with people's perceptions of Israel," he states. "For Jews there always seems to be a double standard" (C. Wecht, personal communication, January 15, 2006).

Michael A. Shochet

Michael Shochet is the Cantor at Rodef Shalom in Falls Church, Virginia. He is also the head police chaplain with the Fairfax County Police Department. Before he was a cantor he was a cop.

Growing up in an upper-class Maryland suburb, the son of a doctor, Shochet had always been interested in becoming either a cop or a cantor. For some reason he always felt that these two things were "in his blood" or were a "part of his psyche." He wanted to help people in a one-on-one fashion, and he wanted to sing Jewish music. In fact, the love of singing Jewish music was his major attraction to Judaism (M. Shochet, personal communication, January 6, 2006).

His family rabbi, who he was very close with, advised Shochet that being a cop would be a step down for a young Jewish boy, that it was not a career for a Jew. There was a tremendous amount of pressure and expectation on him to be a professional, a doctor or a lawyer. But this was not for him. He knew that it was up to him to make the decision about what to do with the rest of his life. At Ithaca college Shochet majored in television production with the aim of being a crime reporter. Nobody thought this was right for him either, except him.

After completing an internship with ABC in Baltimore, Shochet was hired by WMAR Television as a crime reporter. He enjoyed reporting about crime and the police and being "in the thick of things." He decided to combine his love for reporting with his sense of adventure and become a police officer with the goal of being the public information officer with the Baltimore city police department. He approached the then chief of Police Bishop Robinson, who agreed to make Shochet the public information officer, but he would have to attend the police academy first and become a regular police officer.

He entered the Baltimore city police academy as the only Jewish recruit in a class of fifty. The other recruits all know that he was Jewish and nobody gave it a second thought. But what did bother them (as well as some of the "brass" in the police department) was that he had been a reporter. Apparently, there have been reporters in the past who got themselves hired in an attempt to obtain inside information regarding police misbehavior, but he was not one of these.

As a cop, he was assigned to the Eastern District in Baltimore which is one of the roughest areas of the city. There was an abundance of crime, drugs, and poverty. He was surprised that he was having such a good time. "All that power, blue lights, sirens, driving fast" was all terribly exciting," he states.

Shochet still loved to sing. At the end of his police shifts he frequently went directly to choir practice – in uniform – at Temple Emanuel in Baltimore. He was the "choir member with a gun" (M. Shochet, personal communication, January 6, 2006).

In August of 1987, the fun dramatically disappeared from police work for Shochet when his partner, Tony Martini, was shot and injured on the job. He decided it was time to take the chief up on his offer to be the public information officer. He learned, however, that the chief of police had resigned to become the Director of Public Safety for the State of Maryland. The new chief knew nothing about the previous agreement to make Shochet the public information officer, so he was stuck being a cop on the street. He resented that his agreement with police department had been broken and he quit the force.

Shochet attended the Hebrew Union College in New York City and Israel to become a cantor. He graduated in 1994 and took his first job as a cantor in New Orleans. He also became a police chaplain with the New Orleans police department. He remained there until 1998 when he left to take his present position as Rodef Shalom's first cantor.

As a cantor, Shochet is a full partner in the clergy team of Temple Rodef Shalom, joining Senior Rabbi Amy M. Schwartzman and Associate Rabbi Marcus L. Burstein in meeting the full pastoral, educational and spiritual needs of the congregation. He directs the music and cultural areas of Rodef Shalom's congregational life leading services, directing the adult and junior choirs, and the congregational band at numerous cultural events, concerts and programs.

Shochet has gained recognition in the Reform Jewish movement through his leadership positions with the American Conference of

Cantors and the Union for Reform Judaism. He has served on the board of trustees and as Vice President of the American Conference of Cantors and co-edited the current lifecycle manual for American Cantorate used in Reform congregations worldwide. Shochet also served for many years on the Reform movement's Joint Commission on Synagogue Music. He focuses his Cantorate on liturgy and teaching, in addition to creating Jewish cultural experiences for his congregation.

He is certified as a Senior Police Chaplain through the International Conference of Police Chaplains (ICPC),. and serves as the senior chaplain coordinator for the Fairfax County Police Department, as well as a chaplain for the Washington Field Office of the Federal Bureau of Investigation. He is also trained in advanced Critical Incident Stress Management and in other areas of pastoral crisis intervention.

A "law enforcement chaplain" is described by the ICPC as being "a clergyperson with special interest and training for providing pastoral care in the high powered and dangerous world of law enforcement . . . The chaplain's ministry provides a source of strength to the law enforcement officers and their families, other department members, the community, and the incarcerated . . . Chaplains listen and participate in the workplace of law enforcement officers with empathy and experience, advising calmly in the midst of turmoil and danger, and offering assistance when appropriate or requested" (ICPC, 2006, p. 1).

Police Chaplain Shochet rides in police cars in uniform, and holds the administrative rank of Major. He responds to any situation where a citizen or police officer may need help. He provides death notifications when needed, and participates in post-shooting debriefings and counseling when requested. "But sometimes just being there is enough," he says.

Should a Jew be a cop? "It's a natural" says Shochet. The teachings of Judaism emphasize caring, compassion, hospitality for strangers, and above all *tikkum olam*, or repairing the world one mitzvah at a time. "That's what police work is really all about" (M. Shochet, personal communication, January 6, 2006).

Elvis Presley

Why is Elvis Presley included here? He was neither Jewish nor in law enforcement, or was he? Elvis's genealogy might not sound exactly biblical, but it is technically Jewish.

Elvis's mother, Gladys Love Smith, was born on April 25, 1912 and married Vernon Presley. Gladys' mother was Octavia Luvenia Mansell (called "Doll" by family and friends), who married Bob Smith. Doll's mother was Martha Tackett, who married White Mansell. Martha's mother (Elvis's great-great grandmother) was Nancy Burdine and married John Mansell. Nancy was Jewish.

Not much is known about the Burdine family, although they likely came from Lithuania around the time of the American Revolution. According to Elvis's third cousin, Oscar Tackett, two of Martha Tackett's brothers, Sidney and Jerome, had Jewish names.

Elvis was the scion of an uninterrupted female line of Jewish women, and according to the Jewish law of matrilineal descent, that would make the King of rock 'n' roll a member of the Tribe.

Had Elvis, who died in 1977, set out to trace his heritage, he could have easily done this by utilizing any of the Jewish genealogical services that have existed during the last 30 years or so. He would not have needed to travel all over Tennessee and Mississippi in search of his roots. But this is exactly what three Canadian filmmakers – Max Wallace, Evan Beloff and Ari Cohen, together with a rabbi and an Orthodox Elvis impersonator named Dan Hartal did. The result was the 76-minute film called "*Schmelvis: Searching for the King's Jewish Roots*" which premiered in New York in 2002 as part of a program commemorating the 25th anniversary of Presley's death.

The story of Elvis' Jewish lineage was noted in Elaine Dundy's 1985 biography, "*Elvis and Gladys.*" The Wall Street Journal cited the book in a 1998 article about a biennial gathering of Elvis fans at the Elvis Inn, a gas station and café outside Jerusalem. That article in turn inspired the filmmakers' quest, which took them from Montreal to Memphis, then to Israel and back.

Elvis Aaron Presley was born in Tupelo Mississippi but spent most of his formative years in the Jewish quarter of Memphis. Elvis was advised by his father, Vernon, and his manager, Col. Tom Parker, to downplay his Jewish ancestry. Elvis' hairdresser and spiritual adviser, Larry Geller, reported that Gladys Presley gave her son the same advice.

From the reports of many people around him, however, if Elvis had understood that having a Jewish great-great-grandmother made him Jewish, he would have become a full-fledged practicing Jew. There is a lot of evidence which points to Elvis' affinity for things Jewish. He reportedly donated hundreds of thousands of dollars to the Memphis Jewish Welfare Fund, and played racquetball late at night at the Memphis Jewish Community Center.

Years after Elvis's mother died, he had a Star of David inscribed on her gravestone. During his final years, Elvis wore a large, gold necklace with a "chai" pendant. He was said to be wearing it when he died at age 42 in the bathroom of his Memphis mansion, Graceland.

The film *Schmelvis* documented various Jewish aspects of Elvis's young life. For example, as a teenager, he received a scholarship to day camp from the Jewish community, and how his mother pushed him son to go to medical school and become "a doctor." Although he had a nose job to make himself look less Jewish, he still loved his matzah ball soup.

Most people do not know that Elvis was technically Jewish, but even less people know that he was also technically a lawman. Elvis had a life-long fascination with police work, guns, and badges, and even asked President Nixon to make him an honorary secret service agent. Elvis did get appointed a Chief Deputy Sheriff of Shelby County, Tennessee in 1970 by Sheriff Roy C. Nixon (no relation to President Nixon). As a duly sworn deputy Sheriff he had the authority to arrest people – an authority he often exercised – to the shock and amazement of the crime-committing citizens of Memphis.

In 1976, the new Sheriff of Shelby County, Tennessee, Billy Ray Schilling, presented Elvis with the Sheriff's Badge # 1, the highest-ranking badge in the county. Elvis's original Chief Deputy's badge with diamonds and rubies is now displayed in the Elvis Presley Museum in Sweden.

Sources

Dundy, E. *Elvis and Gladys*. (2004). Jackson. MS: University Press of Mississippi.

Fitzgerald, J. Wearing a Beard and a Gun. *Southcoast Today*, Feb 17, 1997.

Greenberg, R. *Let's Take Back our Streets*. (1989). New York: Contemporary Books

Koenig, S. (2004) *Personal Communication*. (October 21, 2004).

International Conference of Police Chaplains. (2006). http://icpc4cops.org (retrieved January 5, 2006).

Rayow, S. (2003) *Personal Communication*. (October 1, 2003).

Schlossberg, H. (2006) *Personal Communication*. (February 1, 2006).

Schlossberg, H. *Psychologist with a Gun*. (1974). New York: Coward, McCann & Geoghegan, Inc.

Shochet, M. (2006) *Personal Communication*. (January 6, 2006).

Terman, L.M. *The Measurement of Intelligence*. In A. Anastasi. Psychological Testing (5th ed.). New York: Macmillan, 1982.

Wecht, C. (2006) *Personal Communication*. (January 15, 2006).

http://icpc4cops.org

About the Author

Dr. Jack Kitaeff is a licensed clinical psychologist in Virginia specializing in forensic and police psychology.

He graduated from the City University of New York. His psychology education includes an MS degree in experimental psychology from the State University of New York and a PhD from the University of Mississippi. He completed a clinical psychology internship at Walter Reed Army Medical Center in Washington, D.C., and a residency in psychology at U.S. Dewitt Army Hospital. He served as a psychologist and Major in the United States Army.

His legal education includes a JD degree from the George Mason University School of Law and a legal clerkship with the United States Attorney's Office, Eastern District of Virginia.

Dr. Kitaeff's private practice concentrates on consulting with police and sheriff departments conducting pre-employment psychological screening of law enforcement applicants, fitness-for-duty evaluations, and psychological profiling.

He enjoys teaching and writing about psychology and the law, and has edited a book on Forensic Psychology. He is an adjunct professor of psychology with the University of Maryland, and serves on the faculty of the Washington Center as well. He has appeared on several television and radio programs.

Dr. Kitaeff lives in northern Virginia with his wife, three children, six cats, and a dog.

Printed in the United States
60205LVS00003B/280-297